Green Finance and Investment

Green Infrastructure in the Decade for Delivery

ASSESSING INSTITUTIONAL INVESTMENT

OECD

BETTER POLICIES FOR BETTER LIVES

This document, as well as any data and map included herein, are without prejudice to the status of or sovereignty over any territory, to the delimitation of international frontiers and boundaries and to the name of any territory, city or area.

The statistical data for Israel are supplied by and under the responsibility of the relevant Israeli authorities. The use of such data by the OECD is without prejudice to the status of the Golan Heights, East Jerusalem and Israeli settlements in the West Bank under the terms of international law.

Note by Turkey
The information in this document with reference to "Cyprus" relates to the southern part of the Island. There is no single authority representing both Turkish and Greek Cypriot people on the Island. Turkey recognises the Turkish Republic of Northern Cyprus (TRNC). Until a lasting and equitable solution is found within the context of the United Nations, Turkey shall preserve its position concerning the "Cyprus issue".

Note by all the European Union Member States of the OECD and the European Union
The Republic of Cyprus is recognised by all members of the United Nations with the exception of Turkey. The information in this document relates to the area under the effective control of the Government of the Republic of Cyprus.

Please cite this publication as:
OECD (2020), *Green Infrastructure in the Decade for Delivery: Assessing Institutional Investment*, Green Finance and Investment, OECD Publishing, Paris, *https://doi.org/10.1787/f51f9256-en*.

ISBN 978-92-64-40443-4 (print)
ISBN 978-92-64-92878-7 (pdf)

Green Finance and Investment
ISSN 2409-0336 (print)
ISSN 2409-0344 (online)

Foreword

This is a critical decade for efforts to tackle global climate change and make progress towards the Sustainable Development Goals. The need to accelerate private investment in low-carbon and resilient critical infrastructure is more important than ever. To avoid sowing the seeds for future crises, we need to build back better and build back greener from the current combined health and economic crisis. An increasing focus on infrastructure development by both governments and institutional investors suggests there is growing momentum to scale up green infrastructure investment.

Capitalising on this momentum will require a nuanced understanding of the current landscape of institutional investment in infrastructure. To shed light on this landscape, this report provides a first-of-its-kind empirical mapping of institutional investors' holdings in the infrastructure sector. The report's quantitative analysis anchors expectations on the potential of institutional investment in infrastructure, and provides a baseline to track and measure progress. Based on these findings, the report's qualitative analysis in chapter 3 outlines key levers and policy priorities to scale-up institutional investment in green infrastructure.

Although the potential for institutional investment in infrastructure has long been recognised, data on current investment is fragmented and incomplete. This report endeavours to inform policymaking by plugging information gaps on investment behaviour. The report combines and harmonises commercial data with desk research and rigorous econometric techniques. The resulting dataset allows a detailed, evidence-based understanding of the differences in investment behaviour between types of investors and pinpoints policy actions -- tailored to reflect existing investment patterns and preferences -- to scale up and shift institutional investment in green infrastructure.

Developed by the OECD Secretariat for the *Working Party on Climate Investment and Development* of the *Environmental Policy Committee*, this report builds on the OECD's extensive body of work on the subject. The dataset and investment insights from this report complement the Directorate's work stream on Approaches to Mobilising Institutional Investment in Sustainable Infrastructure. These new insights provide critical input to ongoing work across the organisation on mobilising private investment in low-carbon, resilient infrastructure as well as on the shifting landscape of institutional investment in infrastructure.

This report aims to lay the groundwork for further OECD work on upscaling investment in green infrastructure. Future OECD research could update data in this report to measure progress, provide new insights and facilitate dynamic evidence-based policymaking.

Rodolfo Lacy, Director, Environment Directorate.

Acknowledgements

This report was produced by the OECD Environment Directorate, directed by Rodolfo Lacy, and the Climate, Biodiversity and Water Division, led by Simon Buckle. This report is authored by Dirk Röttgers and Aayush Tandon, under the supervision of Robert Youngman. The authors are grateful to Antoine Cosson and Joséphine Tassy, for providing substantive inputs to the report. In addition, the authors would like to thank Nassera Belkhiter, Elvira Berrueta-Imaz, Pascale Dénoyer, Niels Gaunard, Elodie Prata-Leal and Ines Reale for administrative support and Sama Al Taher Cucci, Beth Del Bourgo and Stephanie Simonin-Edwards for communications. The authors are responsible for any errors.

This report includes insights from in-depth interviews with investors and investor representatives from the Geneva Association, HSBC Asset Management, Nippon Life, Macquarie Infrastructure and Real Assets (MIRA), Pensionskassernes Administration A/S (PKA) and Principles for Responsible Investing (PRI).The authors are grateful for their availability, openness and insights.

This report has benefited from discussions with and reviews from the following OECD experts: Aimee Aguilar Jaber, Geraldine Ang, Timothy Bishop, Simon Buckle, Romain Despalins, Dennis Dlugosch, Alexander Dobrinevski, Kathleen Dominique, Havard Halland, Raphael Jachnik, Mireille Martini, Alejandra Medina (and team), Daniel Nachtigall, Joel Paula, Harry Smythe, Dariusz Stanko and Cecilia Tam. In addition, the authors are extremely grateful for comments received from Michael Sheren (Bank of England).

This report substantially benefitted from the generous support of the Japanese government.

Table of contents

Tables

Figures

Boxes

Abbreviations and acronyms

AIF	Alternative investment fund	MDB	Multilateral development bank
AUM	Assets under management	MLP	Master limited partnership
bn	billion	NAB	National Australia Bank
CBI	Climate bonds initiative	NY	New York
CPI	Climate policy initiative	OECD	Organisation for Economic Co-operation and Development
CEFC	Clean Energy Finance Corporation	OTC	Over the counter
COVID-19	Coronavirus disease	PF	Pension fund
CSP	Concentrated solar power	PKA	Pensionskassernes Administration A/S
DB	Defined benefit	Q2	Quarter 2
DC	Defined contribution	REC	Renewable energy certificate
ESG	Environmental, social and corporate governance	REIT	Real Estate Investment Trusts
ETF	Exchange-traded funds	RVPI	Residual value to paid-in
EU	European Union	PV	Photovoltaic
FAST-Infra	Finance to Accelerate the Sustainable Transition – Infrastructure	SDG	Sustainable Development Goal
FIP	Feed-in premium	SIF	Strategic investment fund
FIT	Feed-in tariff	SPV	Special purpose vehicle
G20	Group of 20	SWF	Sovereign wealth fund
IC	Insurance company	T&D	Transmission and distribution
INVIT	Infrastructure investment trust	tn	trillion
IPP	Independent power producer	USD	United States dollars
LCEG	Low-Carbon Electricity Generation		

Executive summary

Energy, water, transport, health and other infrastructure are critical for socio-economic development. Yet, infrastructure suffers from an estimated annual investment gap of around USD 2.5-3 trillion globally. The on-going public health emergency is a telling reminder of the risks of underinvestment in infrastructure. Among other things, underinvestment compromises our ability to effectively respond to systemic challenges, like climate change.

Given the long lifecycle of infrastructure assets, investment decisions today will have lasting implications for global climate and development trajectories. Delivering on international climate and development goals requires a shift to and scaling up of investments in green infrastructure. However, the COVID-19 crisis exacerbates the pressures on government budgets, revenues and debt that constrain public investment in many countries. Yet the need to mobilise private capital at scale towards critical infrastructure development is urgent.

The importance of institutional investors for infrastructure investment is well recognised. While much effort has been dedicated to increasing institutional investment in infrastructure, it still accounts for only a fraction of institutional portfolios. Persistent low returns on traditional investments like bonds and stocks, however, are motivating investors to look to alternative investments, including infrastructure. The momentum created by this trend, and increasing interest in sustainability among institutional investors, presents an opportunity to scale up institutional investment in green infrastructure.

A nuanced understanding of the current investment landscape and investment preferences is key to accelerate and shift institutional investment in green infrastructure. To address knowledge gaps in these areas, the three chapters of this report make the following key contributions:

- An estimate of **investable assets under management (AUM) of institutional investors** (pension funds and insurance companies) to anchor expectations around institutional investment in infrastructure development;
- A first-of its kind comprehensive **empirical mapping of current holdings (i.e. stock, not flows) of infrastructure investment by institutional investors**, from OECD and G20 countries; and
- An **analytical framework** highlighting the key levers and identifying policy priorities to scale-up institutional investment in green infrastructure.

For the purpose of the empirical analysis, this report adopts a pragmatic definition of green infrastructure. Given the lack of a widely accepted definition of green infrastructure, the adopted definition is based on a comparative analysis of multiple regulatory approaches, including the EU sustainable finance taxonomy.

This report finds that under current investment regulations in OECD and G20 countries, pension funds and insurance companies can allocate a **maximum of USD 11.4 trillion towards infrastructure (investable AUM)**. This estimate should be treated as a theoretical regulatory upper bound. This estimate is far higher than institutional investors' current investments, and suggests that regulatory limits are generally not a constraint. It also suggests that simply "fixing the regulation" will not be sufficient in itself to trigger massive institutional investment in the infrastructure sector.

Close to 60% of the urban infrastructure to exist by 2030 is yet to be built, so this report focuses on how to maximise the positive impact of institutional investments on the real economy. Thus, the bulk of the analysis is **focused on holdings through unlisted funds, project-level equity and debt as well as securitised products** with direct exposure to real assets. For completeness and comparison, the empirical mapping also tracks investment in infrastructure-related corporate stocks.

As the empirical mapping of this report shows, institutional investors hold **USD 1.04 trillion in infrastructure assets** (excluding direct investment in corporate stocks). Of this, **USD 314 billion (30%) are attributed to green infrastructure**.

Other key findings of the empirical investigation of institutional investment in infrastructure include:

- Infrastructure allocations by **asset owners** target **long-term capital appreciation**. The majority of investments are held in **illiquid assets** offering an illiquidity premium.
- Conversely, **asset managers** demonstrate a **preference for liquidity** in their allocations. The majority of investments are held through **securitised products** like YieldCos, REITs and INVITs. Notably, 49% of all institutional investment in *green* infrastructure is held through YieldCos alone.
- Persistent low yields on traditional financial products and a **rising risk appetite** of asset owners suggest **increased availability of construction stage capital** going forward.
- Institutional investors exhibit a strong preference for assets located within their own regions.
- Cross-border institutional investment mainly targets assets located in **mature markets**.

Findings from the empirical mapping help identify levers and policy actions to shift and scale up institutional investment in green infrastructure. The analytical framework developed here highlights three pathways:

To address the lack of sufficient investment-grade projects, governments can scale up **green project pipelines**. For investors, the costs of building capacity are difficult to justify for one-off investments. If they have greater certainty that follow-on projects will be available, investors would be better able to gauge risks, invest in capacity building and help foster a market for infrastructure investment. Additionally, increasing the supply of investment-grade projects could help address currently high project valuations. Partnerships between investors and governments can also provide an effective way to share risks, achieve scale and establish a pipeline of investment-grade projects.

Mandates issued by asset owners offer a key pathway to scale up green infrastructure investments through unlisted funds. Asset owners' selection of asset managers and investment consultants is critical to integrating climate and development objectives in investment decisions. Actions by regulators to clarify the relationship between fiduciary duty, duty of care and consideration of climate-related risks could encourage asset owners to issue "green" mandates.

Securitised products could appeal to investors with a preference for liquidity. In particular, securitisation could benefit from a shift towards defined contribution pension plans as well as passive investment and enlarge the investor base for infrastructure assets. In jurisdictions where regulators permit them, YieldCos, infrastructure REITs and INVITs, could be useful products in this regard.

Beyond these three pathways, the establishment of more precise and consistent definitions of which investments are "green" could facilitate investment by giving confidence and assurance to investors. A common understanding of 'green' and 'sustainable' infrastructure would accelerate investment flows by simplifying due diligence and investment decision making.

Institutional investors are increasingly conscious of the environmental impact of their investments, and are increasingly looking to make green investments. As governments and the private sector seek to 'build back better' and ensure a green recovery, this is an opportune moment for green infrastructure development. However, it will take committed and innovative policies to expedite investment flows towards green infrastructure.

1 Green Infrastructure in the decade for delivery

Infrastructure investment is key to economic growth, meeting climate and sustainable development goals, and ensuring resilience to systemic challenges like the COVID-19 crisis and climate change. Yet, infrastructure investments globally fall USD 2.5 – 3 trillion short of estimated annual needs, and remain misaligned with climate mitigation and resilience goals. This report provides detailed empirical analysis of current infrastructure holdings by institutional investors, and explores in greater depth promising instruments to scale up green infrastructure investment.

Energy, water, health and other infrastructure are critical for the socio-economic development of our societies. Infrastructure systems form the backbone of our economies and their availability and quality are important determinants of collective well-being. Yet, the sector suffers from declining investment globally in both developed and developing countries. The recent COVID-19 public health emergency is a telling reminder of the risks of underinvestment in essential infrastructure. Among other things, underinvestment in infrastructure can compromise the economy's ability to effectively respond to systemic challenges.

At present, global infrastructure faces an investment gap of some USD 2.5-3 trillion annually (OECD/The World Bank/UN Environment, 2018[1]). Despite infrastructure cost-reductions achieved through technological advancement, infrastructure investment continues to fall short of annual needs, enlarging the aggregate deficit. Annually, an estimated USD 6.3 trillion is needed in total infrastructure investments through 2030. The lion's share - USD 4 trillion - is required in developing and emerging economies (NCE, 2016[2]). Emerging Asia[1] alone needs investments of USD 1.7 trillion yearly to ensure sustained socio-economic development (ADB, 2017[3]). With 60% of global population projected to live in urban areas by 2030, 60% of the urban infrastructure needed is yet to be built (UN, 2018[4]).

Building 'green' to ensure economic and social well-being

Infrastructure plays a central role in meeting climate as well as wider environmental and development objectives. Energy, transport and water infrastructure together are responsible for 60% of global carbon emissions (OECD/The World Bank/UN Environment, 2018[1]). Current practices in developing and using infrastructure are accelerating environmental degradation, including through greenhouse gas emissions, air and water pollution, waste production and biodiversity loss. Given the long lifecycle of infrastructure assets, investment decisions today will have lasting implications for long-term emissions as well as the ability of the wider system to achieve the sustainable development goals (SDGs[2]). The combined emissions intensity of existing and planned infrastructure implies that all infrastructure going forward must be aligned with emission reduction targets to be able to deliver on global climate commitments (Hepburn et al., 2020[5]; Smith et al., 2019[6]). The lack of resilience in current infrastructure assets (Koks et al., 2019[7]; Nicolas et al., 2019[8]) has generated substantial extant costs. This points to an imminent need to adapt the current as well as future stock of infrastructure to weather the effects of climate change.

Infrastructure investments form an essential component of COVID-19 recovery packages provided by governments. The potential for rising momentum behind private-sector infrastructure investing coupled with an increased willingness from the public sector to support projects provides a critical opportunity to *build back better* (OECD, 2020[9]).

The benefits of green infrastructure come at a marginal increase in total cost.

The OECD estimates it would take only a 10% increase in yearly investment (from USD 6.3 trillion to USD 6.9 trillion[3]) to develop infrastructure aligned with the goals of the Paris agreement (OECD, 2017[10]). The incremental investment, driven to a large degree by decarbonisation of the energy sector, is low compared with the benefits of avoiding long-term high-carbon growth trajectory. Timely investment in green infrastructure[4] can generate up to USD 4.1 trillion in net benefits by 2030 (Global Commission on Adaptation, 2019[11]). This investment would also be more than offset by savings from forgone fossil fuel expenditure (USD 1.6 trillion per year) (OECD, 2017[10]; NCE, 2014[12]).

While the economic case for additional public and private investment in infrastructure is clear, shrinking fiscal space and debt ceilings in many countries is increasingly constraining public sector investment. As we enter the 'decade of delivery' of global climate and development commitments from 2020-2030, the imperative to mobilise private capital is stronger than ever.

Both the public and private sector have made efforts to increase private investment in infrastructure[5]. Nevertheless, the scale and pace of investment falls far short of what is required to ensure sustainable and inclusive growth. The private sector accounted for only 17% of global infrastructure investments in 2017 (World Bank, 2017[13]). Going forward, infrastructure development will increasingly be dependent on successful mobilisation of private finance. Given the size of their assets under management, institutional investors[6] represent an important, even essential, pool of capital for scaling up infrastructure investment.

Institutional investors and green infrastructure development

Several factors suggest there is a significant opportunity to increase institutional investment in infrastructure

In recent years, low risk-adjusted returns on traditional assets like stocks and bonds have increasingly led institutional investors to pivot towards alternative investments, including infrastructure (CIBC Mellon, 2019[14]), which can be a useful choice to match long-term assets to long-term liabilities. For pension funds, persistent low yields only amplify the need to invest in higher yielding alternatives to overcome funding gaps (World Economic Forum, 2017[15]). This is especially true given the increased pressure on pension funds through lower returns as a result of the COVID-19 crisis (Allianz, 2020[16]) as well as generally in countries with persistent funding gaps such as the United Kingdom and the United States (OECD, 2018[17]; OECD, 2019[18]). Infrastructure assets that offer long-term, stable and inflation linked cash flows align well with the long-dated liabilities of such investors. According to a recent survey by EDHEC Infra and the Global Infrastructure Hub, 79% of surveyed investors[7] intend to increase their allocation to infrastructure over the period 2020-2023 (EDHEC Infrastructure Institute-Singapore, 2019[19]). This trend, together with rising institutional interest in sustainable investing (KPMG, AIMA, CAIA, 2020[20]), suggests that green infrastructure has the potential to fulfil return expectations of institutional investors.

But progress requires a granular understanding of current investments

The role that institutional investors can play in global infrastructure development is well documented (Della Croce, 2014[21]; Röttgers, Tandon and Kaminker, 2018[22]; Della Croce, 2011[23]). Several organisations, including the OECD, have further identified and analysed the modalities to direct institutional capital towards infrastructure (OECD, 2015[24]; Inderst, 2016[25]; Nelson and Pierpont, 2013[26]; Della Croce and Yermo, 2013[27]; Youngman and Kaminker, 2016[28]; Inderst, 2016[29]; Kaminker, 2016[30]; G20/OECD, 2013[31]). These analyses particularly point out institutional investors' role as 'recyclers of capital', taking operational assets off balance sheets of short-term financiers, thereby freeing up capital for new investment.

Despite much research in recent years on institutional investors' potential to expand investment in infrastructure, progress to date appears to be marginal (G20/OECD, 2019[32]). Deeper analysis and evaluation of how to mobilise institutional investment in infrastructure has been constrained by the lack of granular data and information on institutional investment in infrastructure. This is especially true for current holdings and on non-green investments. A number of fundamental questions remain partially or fully unanswered: How much is invested? Through which instruments and vehicles? Into which sectors? In and from which regions?

Efforts to shift institutional investment towards infrastructure require a concrete quantitative assessment of how much can be shifted as well as to which types of investments. More precise knowledge of the current investment landscape can: (i) permit in-depth and detailed diagnostics; (ii) provide a more reliable and granular evidence base to guide policymaking; and (iii) help devise investment options and rationales targeted to specific investor categories and attributes. This quantitative assessment of current and potential investment would of course have to be interpreted in the context of more qualitative factors. Importantly, beyond potential for growth in specific investment channels, investments have to be in the best interest of savers, i.e. have a risk-return and other characteristics that fulfil fiduciary duty.

This report presents OECD's latest efforts to map, as comprehensively as possible, current institutional holdings in infrastructure, i.e. their stock of investment. The mapping provides first of its kind detail and aims to plug crucial data gaps identified in the literature (G20, 2018[33]), The quantitative exercise conducted for this report contributes to wider efforts to enhance data quality and availability (Global Infrastructure Hub - Quality Infrastructure Database, 2020[34]; Private Participation in Infrastructure (PPI) - World Bank Group, 2020[35]; Infrastructure Data Initiative, 2020[36]). Results of the quantitative mapping are presented in Chapter 2, with methodological notes in the chapter's Annex. Notwithstanding these efforts to provide a comprehensive mapping, important data gaps remain, as discussed in Chapter 2.

And a more realistic expectation of the role institutional investors can play

Institutional investors in OECD and G20 countries have at least USD 64.8 trillion[8] in assets under management (AUM) -- a measure against which policies and other mobilisation efforts are often evaluated. However, considerations regarding diversification, portfolio concentration, fiscal stability (as institutional investors are holders of government bonds) and quantitative limits on asset allocation (for pension funds and insurance companies) mean that not all AUM are available for infrastructure investments.

Developing effective and targeted mobilisation efforts requires a more nuanced frame of reference than high-level estimates of AUM. Regulations governing investment activities of institutional investors are a good starting point. This report has developed an estimate[9] of the maximum institutional capital that, in theory, could be channelled towards infrastructure investments given current regulations ("investable AUM").

Given the regulatory framework in OECD and G20 countries, pension funds and insurance companies can allocate at most ca. USD 11.4 trillion through unlisted funds or directly through project-level equity and debt. These instruments are central given their potential to direct capital to the real economy (new asset finance as well as refinancing and acquisition of operational assets), and are the focus for asset owners-related analysis of this report. The estimated USD 11.4 trillion highlight the amount that will be available for infrastructure, if pension funds and insurance companies invested the maximum amount they are allowed to invest through unlisted funds, project-level equity and project-level debt in infrastructure. Investing the entire investable AUM in infrastructure is of course unlikely given the need for portfolio diversification (OECD, 2019[37]; OECD, 2015[38]). Further, quantitative limits prescribed in certain jurisdictions do not distinguish between infrastructure and other assets that can be accessed through unlisted instruments. This means that part of the USD 11.4 trillion is likely to be invested in assets other than infrastructure e.g. private equity, hedge funds etc.

Figure 1.1. Breakdown of Investable AUM and the share of Infrastructure Investment

Source: Authors

In spite of this caveat, an estimate of investable AUM advances the discussion in two important ways:

First, estimated investable AUM provides a more accurate reference point to measure progress and anchor expectations around the role of institutional investors. To illustrate, according to the empirical work undertaken for this report, (presented in Chapter 2) current infrastructure investment by pension funds and insurance companies through unlisted funds and direct investments amounts to USD 450 billion. This equals 4.1 % of the investable AUM under current regulatory limits. However, it amounts to a mere 0.7% if measured against the total AUM – a figure that includes assets that cannot be invested in unlisted infrastructure under present regulations.

Second, there is plenty of room to expand infrastructure investment under current investment limits. The estimate of investable AUM suggests that extant regulations governing investment activities of pension funds and insurance companies generally is not a significant limiting factor for infrastructure investment. In the majority of countries, limits exceed the currently invested capital by far. Institutional investment in infrastructure has appreciable room to grow within the confines set by current regulations.

Regulations beyond investment limits in some jurisdictions may indeed hamper institutional infrastructure investment. Some regulation of institutional investment, e.g. the EU's Solvency II regulation on capital requirements of insurance companies, tend to be singled out as barriers to institutional investment as they may constrain capital flows to these investments (HSBC, 2019[39]; IEIF, 2019[40]). However, there is no reason to believe that simply "fixing the regulation" on its own will trigger massive institutional investment or specifically an influx of institutional capital into the infrastructure sector. Hence in addition to an analysis of regulatory barriers, it is key to investigate more effective market-based instruments and commensurate policy measures (see Chapter 3 for details).

The estimate above appears to be the first estimate of its type. It focuses on unlisted instruments given their potential to direct capital to the real economy. Further research could refine and improve the estimate, e.g. by investigating the debt and equity distribution within the investable AUM for direct project-level investments. The underlying methodology might also be leveraged to develop annual estimates.

Structure of the report

The rest of the report is structured as follows:

Chapter 2 presents the results of the empirical mapping undertaken for this report, including pragmatic definitions used for the purpose of this report of *infrastructure* and *green*. The new data developed and presented in chapter 2 allows a detailed assessment of the investment behaviour of asset owners and managers.

Guided by the findings in chapter 2, chapter 3 develops an analytical framework to identify levers and policy priorities to scale-up institutional investment in green infrastructure. This chapter incorporates insights from six in-depth interviews with stakeholders representing institutional investors.

Annex 1.A. **Estimating Investable AUM of Institutional Investors**

Investment activities of institutional investors are regulated in most OECD and G20 jurisdictions. Requirements regarding diversification, concentration and quantitative and qualitative[10] limits on asset allocation mean that not all assets under management (AUM) will be available for infrastructure investments. To inform policymaking and analysis to catalyse institutional investment in sustainable infrastructure, this report provides estimates of the maximum institutional capital that, in theory, could be channelled towards infrastructure investments given current regulations. Framing investment mobilisation efforts in the context of such a maximum bound can: (i) allow a more accurate assessment of progress; (ii) provide direction to such efforts; and (iii) anchor expectations around the role of institutional investors including expectations regarding specific types of institutional investors.

These estimates are based on investment regulations in OECD and G20 countries. Regulations around investment activities of pension funds and insurance companies can be grouped broadly into: (i) those prescribing *quantitative and qualitative limits* on portfolio allocation into specific asset categories; and (ii) those prescribing the *prudent person principle* or a similar risk-based investment management principle.

Further, investments are often regulated by specific asset classes. Certain instrument and vehicles are more suited than others to channel infrastructure investments in the real economy, i.e. providing funds for new asset finance and refinancing and acquisition of operational assets. As **unlisted funds** and **direct project-level equity and debt** are primary asset classes for investments in the real economy, this report only provides estimates for capital that can be provided through these asset classes. The estimations are based on OECD records of quantitative limits, and uses industry data where necessary to cover jurisdictions which prescribe the *prudent person principle*.

Methodology for investments through Unlisted Funds

For investors domiciled in jurisdictions that prescribe *quantitative limits*[11] on portfolio allocation, the limit[12] provided for private investment funds is applied. Where available, the estimation uses the limit on alternative investment funds (AIFs) or infrastructure investment funds instead, as it is more specific to infrastructure.

For actors domiciled in jurisdictions that do not prescribe asset-specific limits, the highest known 'infrastructure allocation target'[13] used by pension funds or insurance companies in a given country is applied[14]. The estimation takes the highest 'infrastructure allocation target' as a proxy for industry prudence given prevailing regulatory climate, business structures and risk-return preferences in that country. Where data on target allocation is unavailable, the estimation approach uses the highest known 'allocation to infrastructure'[15] (as a percentage of total allocations) instead.

Annex Figure 1.A.1. Methodology Overview

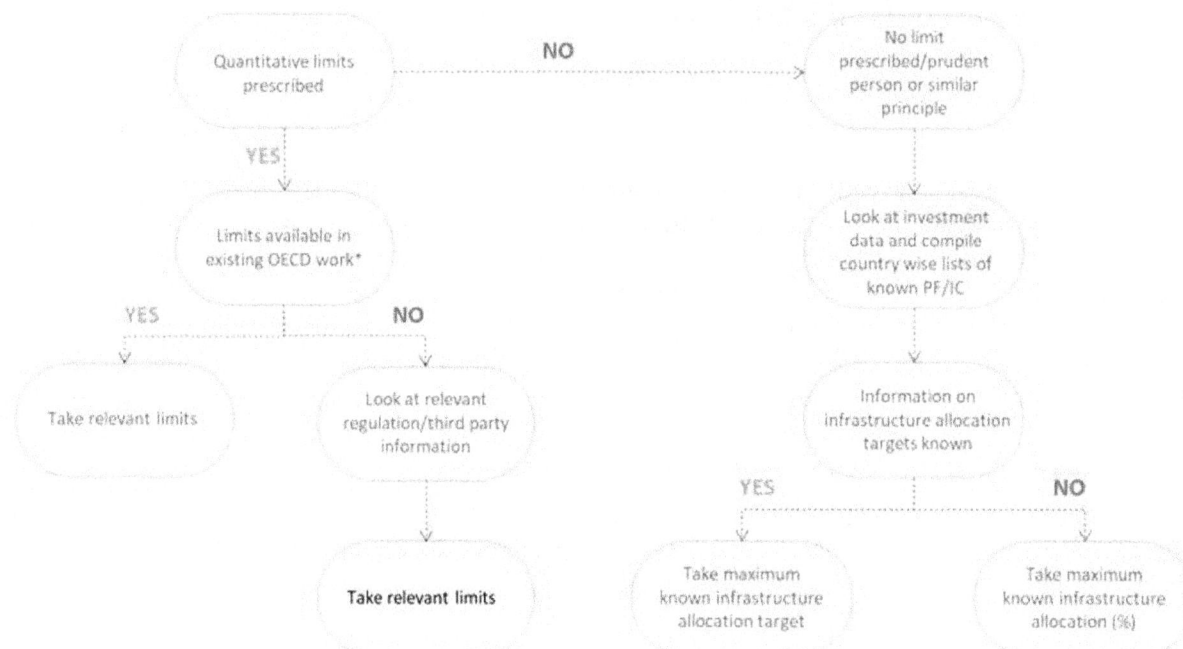

Note: PF: Pension Funds
IC: Insurance Companies
*http://www.oecd.org/daf/fin/private-pensions/2019-Survey-Investment-Regulation-Pension-Funds.pdf;
https://www.oecd.org/g20/summits/antalya/Regulation-of-Insurance-Company-and-Pension-Fund-Investment.pdf
Source: Authors

Methodology for investments through Direct Project-Level Investments

For investors domiciled in jurisdictions that prescribe quantitative limits[16], the estimation applies the limits provided for investment through unlisted equity. Where available, the limit on investment in Special Purpose Vehicles (SPVs) or similar structures is chosen instead, as it is more clearly associated with infrastructure investment. Where neither of these limits is available, the limit on private investment funds is used.

For actors domiciled in jurisdictions that prescribe the prudent person principle (for instance under Solvency II), the estimation employs a best in class approach. The best in class approach takes the highest known 'infrastructure allocation target'[17] by pension funds or insurance companies in a given country. The estimation takes the highest 'infrastructure allocation target' as a proxy for industry prudence given prevailing regulatory climate, business structures and risk-return preferences in that country. Where data on target allocation is unavailable, the highest known 'allocation to infrastructure'18 (as a percentage of total allocations) is chosen instead.

References

(n.a.) (2019), *PENSION MARKETS IN FOCUS.* [50]

ADB (2017), *MEETING ASIA'S INFRASTRUCTURE NEEDS*, Asian Development Bank, Manila, [3]
https://www.adb.org/sites/default/files/publication/227496/special-report-infrastructure.pdf
(accessed on 29 April 2020).

Allianz (2020), *Allianz Pension Report 2020*, Allianz, [16]
https://www.allianz.com/content/dam/onemarketing/azcom/Allianz_com/economic-
research/publications/specials/en/2020/mai/Allianz_Global_Pension_Report_2020.pdf.

CIBC Mellon (2019), *The Race for Assets*, https://www.cibcmellon.com/en/_locale- [14]
assets/pdf/our-thinking/2019/the-cibc-mellon-race-for-assets-canada-vs-world-may-2019.pdf
(accessed on 30 April 2020).

Della Croce, R. (2014), *I.6. ARE INSTITUTIONAL INVESTORS THE ANSWER FOR LONG-* [21]
TERM DEVELOPMENT FINANCING?, OECD Publishing , Paris,
http://dx.doi.org/10.1787/888933121601.

Della Croce, R. (2011), *Pension Funds Investment in Infrastructure: Policy Actions*, [51]
https://www.oecd-ilibrary.org/finance-and-investment/pension-funds-investment-in-
infrastructure_5kg272f9bnmx-en (accessed on 26 May 2020).

Della Croce, R. (2011), "Pension Funds Investment in Infrastructure: Policy Actions", *OECD* [23]
Working Papers on Finance, Insurance and Private Pensions, No. 13, OECD Publishing,
Paris, https://dx.doi.org/10.1787/5kg272f9bnmx-en.

Della Croce, R. and J. Yermo (2013), "Institutional Investors and Infrastructure Financing", [27]
OECD Working Papers on Finance, Insurance and Private Pensions, No. 36, OECD
Publishing, Paris, https://dx.doi.org/10.1787/5k3wh99xgc33-en.

EDHEC (2020), *2020Q1 Index Release: Covid-19 lockdown highlights the importance of* [48]
understanding risk in unlisted infrastructure investments,
https://edhec.infrastructure.institute/announcement/ (accessed on 28 May 2020).

EDHEC Infrastructure Institute-Singapore, G. (2019), *A Publication of the EDHEC Infrastructure* [19]
Institute-Singapore 2019 Global Infrastructure Investor Survey Benchmarking Trends and
Best Practices, https://cdn.gihub.org/umbraco/media/2564/global-infrastructure-investor-
survey-report-2019.pdf (accessed on 29 April 2020).

Energy Agency, I. and I. Renewable Energy Agency (n.d.), "PERSPECTIVES FOR THE [56]
ENERGY TRANSITION Investment Needs for a Low-Carbon Energy System About the IEA",
https://www.energiewende2017.com/wp-content/uploads/2017/03/Perspectives-for-the-
Energy-Transition_WEB.pdf (accessed on 4 December 2017).

European Union (n.d.), *Recovery plan for Europe*, 2020, https://ec.europa.eu/info/live-work- [59]
travel-eu/health/coronavirus-response/recovery-plan-europe_en.

G20 (2019), *G20 Osaka Leaders' Declaration*, [45]
https://www.mofa.go.jp/policy/economy/g20_summit/osaka19/en/documents/final_g20_osaka
_leaders_declaration.html (accessed on 29 April 2020).

G20 (2019), *G20 PRINCIPLES FOR QUALITY INFRASTRUCTURE INVESTMENT*, https://www.mof.go.jp/english/international_policy/convention/g20/annex6_1.pdf (accessed on 29 April 2020). [44]

G20 (2018), *ROADMAP TO INFRASTRUCTURE AS AN ASSET CLASS Infrastructure for Growth and Development*, https://cdn.gihub.org/umbraco/media/2572/roadmap-to-infrastructure-as-an-asset-class-50.pdf (accessed on 29 April 2020). [33]

G20/OECD (2019), *Annual Survey of Large Pension Funds and Public Pension Reserve Funds*, G20/OECD, http://www.oecd.org/finance/survey-large-pension-funds.htm (accessed on 26 May 2020). [54]

G20/OECD (2019), *ANNUAL SURVEY OF LARGE PENSION FUNDS AND PUBLIC PENSION RESERVE FUNDS REPORT ON PENSION FUNDS' LONG-TERM INVESTMENTS*, http://www.oecd.org/finance/survey-large-pension-funds.htm (accessed on 20 July 2020). [32]

G20/OECD (2013), *High-level principles of long-term investment financing by institutional investors*, http://www.oecd.org (accessed on 18 June 2020). [31]

Global Commission on Adaptation (2019), *ADAPT NOW: A GLOBAL CALL FOR LEADERSHIP ON CLIMATE RESILIENCE #AdaptOurWorld*. [11]

Global Infrastructure Hub - Quality Infrastructure Database (2020), *Global Infrastructure Hub - Quality Infrastructure Database*, https://www.gihub.org/quality-infrastructure-database (accessed on 29 April 2020). [34]

Hepburn, C. et al. (2020), "Committed Emissions from Existing and Planned Power Plants and Asset Stranding Required to Meet the Paris Agreement", https://econpapers.repec.org/RePEc:idb:brikps:8886 (accessed on 17 July 2020). [5]

HSBC (2019), *European Commission proposes reduced capital charges for qualifying equities and fixed income assets*, https://www.assetmanagement.hsbc.fr/-/media/files/attachments/uk/common/amgb-ar-solvency-ii-update-03-2019.pdf. [39]

IEA (2020), *World Energy Investment 2020*, International Energy Agency, Paris, https://dx.doi.org/10.1787/6f552938-en. [47]

IEIF (2019), *IEIF | Reforming Solvency II for insurers could trigger 'Big Bang' for European listed real estate and lead to surge in investment capital flows*, https://www.ieif.fr/revue_de_presse/reforming-solvency-ii-for-insurers-could-trigger-big-bang-for-european-listed-real-estate-and-lead-to-surge-in-investment-capital-flows (accessed on 26 May 2020). [40]

Inderst, G. (2016), "Infrastructure Investment, Private Finance, and Institutional Investors: Asia from a Global Perspective", *SSRN Electronic Journal*, http://dx.doi.org/10.2139/ssrn.2721577. [53]

Inderst, G. (2016), "Infrastructure Investment, Private Finance, and Institutional Investors: Asia from a Global Perspective", *SSRN Electronic Journal*, http://dx.doi.org/10.2139/ssrn.2721577. [25]

Inderst, G. (2016), "Infrastructure Investment, Private Finance, and Institutional Investors: Asia from a Global Perspective", *SSRN Electronic Journal*, http://dx.doi.org/10.2139/ssrn.2721577. [29]

Infrastructure Data Initiative (2020), *Infrastructure Data Initiative*, [36]
https://www.gihub.org/resources/data/infrastructure-data-initiative/ (accessed on
29 April 2020).

IRENA (2017), *Perspectives for the energy transition: Investment needs for a low-carbon energy* [42]
system.

Kaminker, C. (2016), "Progress Report on Approaches to Mobilising Institutional Investment for [52]
Green Infrastructure", OECD, Paris.

Kaminker, C. (2016), "Progress Report on Approaches to Mobilising Institutional Investment for [30]
Green Infrastructure", OECD, Paris.

Koks, E. et al. (2019), "A global multi-hazard risk analysis of road and railway infrastructure [7]
assets", http://dx.doi.org/10.1038/s41467-019-10442-3.

KPMG, AIMA, CAIA (2020), *Sustainable investing: fast-forwarding its evolution*, [20]
https://assets.kpmg/content/dam/kpmg/xx/pdf/2020/02/sustainable-investing.pdf (accessed on
30 April 2020).

Mirabile, M. and J. Calder (2018), "Clean power for a cool planet: Electricity infrastructure plans [41]
and the Paris Agreement", *OECD Environment Working Papers*, No. 140, OECD Publishing,
Paris, https://dx.doi.org/10.1787/2dc84376-en.

NCE (2016), *THE SUSTAINABLE INFRASTRUCTURE IMPERATIVE Financing for Better* [2]
Growth and Development THE 2016 NEW CLIMATE ECONOMY REPORT, New Climate
Economy, http://www.newclimateeconomy.report (accessed on 29 April 2020).

NCE (2014), *THE SYNTHESIS REPORT SEPTEMBER 2014 THE GLOBAL COMMISSION ON* [12]
THE ECONOMY AND CLIMATE BETTER GROWTH BETTER CLIMATE THE SYNTHESIS
REPORT, New Climate Economy, http://www.newclimateeconomy.report (accessed on
29 April 2020).

Nelson, D. and B. Pierpont (2013), "The Challenge of Institutional Investment in Renewable [26]
Energy CPI Report Climate Policy Initiative".

Nicolas, C. et al. (2019), *STRONGER POWER Improving Power Sector Resilience to Natural* [8]
Hazards LIFELINES: The Resilient Infrastructure Opportunity, http://www.worldbank.org
(accessed on 29 April 2020).

OECD (2020), *Building Back Better: A Sustainable, Resilient Recovery after Covid-19 - OECD*, [9]
https://read.oecd-ilibrary.org/view/?ref=133_133639-s08q2ridhf&title=Building-back-better-_A-
sustainable-resilient-recovery-after-Covid-19 (accessed on 20 July 2020).

OECD (2020), *From containment to recovery: Environmental responses to the COVID-19* [49]
pandemic, https://read.oecd-ilibrary.org/view/?ref=126_126460-1tg1r2aowf&title=From-
containment-to-recovery_Environmental-responses-to-the-COVID-19-pandemic (accessed on
26 May 2020).

OECD (2020), *OECD Economic Outlook, Volume 2020 Issue 1*, OECD Publishing, Paris, [58]
https://dx.doi.org/10.1787/0d1d1e2e-en.

OECD (2019), *Annual survey of investment regulation of pension funds*, OECD, Paris, http://www.oecd.org/daf/fin/private-pensions/2019-Survey-Investment-Regulation-Pension-Funds.pdf. [37]

OECD (2019), *Pension markets in focus*. [18]

OECD (2018), *Pension Markets in Focus*, http://www.oecd.org/daf/pensions/pensionmarkets. (accessed on 26 May 2020). [17]

OECD (2017), *Investing in Climate, Investing in Growth*, OECD Publishing, Paris, https://dx.doi.org/10.1787/9789264273528-en. [10]

OECD (2017), "Investment governance and the integration of environmental, social and governance factors". [46]

OECD (2015), *Mapping Channels to Mobilise Institutional Investment in Sustainable Energy*, Green Finance and Investment, OECD Publishing, Paris, https://dx.doi.org/10.1787/9789264224582-en. [24]

OECD (2015), *Regulation of insurance company and pension fund investment*, OECD, Paris, https://www.oecd.org/g20/summits/antalya/Regulation-of-Insurance-Company-and-Pension-Fund-Investment.pdf. [38]

OECD/The World Bank/UN Environment (2018), *Financing Climate Futures: Rethinking Infrastructure*, OECD Publishing, Paris, https://dx.doi.org/10.1787/9789264308114-en. [1]

Preqin (2020), *Alternative Assets Data, Solutions and Insights*. [57]

Private Participation in Infrastructure (PPI) - World Bank Group (2020), *Private Participation in Infrastructure (PPI) - World Bank Group*, https://ppi.worldbank.org/en/ppi (accessed on 29 April 2020). [35]

Puig, D. et al. (2016), *General rights The Adaptation Finance Gap Report*, United Nations Environment Programme, http://www.unep.org/climatechange/adaptation/gapreport2016/ (accessed on 29 April 2020). [55]

Röttgers, D., A. Tandon and C. Kaminker (2018), "OECD Progress Update on Approaches to Mobilising Institutional Investment for Sustainable Infrastructure", *OECD Environment Working Papers*, No. 138, OECD Publishing, Paris, https://dx.doi.org/10.1787/45426991-en. [22]

Smith, C. et al. (2019), "Current fossil fuel infrastructure does not yet commit us to 1.5 C warming", *Nature*, https://www.nature.com/articles/s41467-018-07999-w?fbclid=IwAR06X-jqZT5jRddBiLf2j_n4LjexWpJ1viWm2UuO5SiHQzl63vVouozvexE (accessed on 17 July 2020). [6]

UN (2018), *The World's Cities in 2018- Data Booklet*, United Nations, Department of Economic and Social Affairs, Population Division, https://www.un.org/en/events/citiesday/assets/pdf/the_worlds_cities_in_2018_data_booklet.pdf (accessed on 30 April 2020). [4]

UNEP (2016), *The Adaptation Finance Gap Report*, United Nations Environment Programme (UNEP), Nairobi, https://unepdtu.org/publications/the-adaptation-finance-gap-report/. [43]

World Bank (2017), *WHO SPONSORS INFRASTRUCTURE PROJECTS? Acknowledgement* [13]
& *Disclaimer*, The World Bank Group,
https://ppi.worldbank.org/content/dam/PPI/documents/SPIReport_2017_small_interactive.pdf
(accessed on 29 April 2020).

World Economic Forum (2017), *We'll Live to 100-How Can We Afford It?*, World Economic [15]
Forum, http://www3.weforum.org/docs/WEF_White_Paper_We_Will_Live_to_100.pdf
(accessed on 30 April 2020).

Youngman, R. and C. Kaminker (2016), "Institutional investors and green infrastructure [28]
investment: OECD report for the climate finance ministerial meeting", *OECD Climate Finance
Ministerial*.

Notes

[1] A set of 45 Asian countries as listed in appendix 4.4 in ADB (2017[3]), excluding Japan, but including the OECD and G20 countries China, India, Indonesia and Korea.

[2] For a full list of the UN Sustainable Development Goals, see https://sdgs.un.org/goals.

[3] Under an IEA scenario achieving 2 degrees with 66% probability.

[4] Note that green infrastructure includes low-carbon and resilient infrastructure. Please see chapter 2 for the more detailed ad-hoc definition this report uses in the empirical analysis.

[5] For example the Climate Investment Coalition (https://www.climateinvestmentcoalition.org/), the Institutional Investor Group on Climate Change and the Net-Zero Asset Owners Alliance (https://www.unepfi.org/net-zero-alliance/alliance-members/).

[6] Unless stated otherwise the term "institutional investors" include pension funds (public and private), insurance companies (life and general) and sovereign wealth funds.

[7] The survey includes responses for 300 asset owners and managers. 130 asset owners with a combined AUM of USD 10 trillion participated in the survey.

[8] Based on (Preqin, 2020[57]) and authors' research, based on pension fund and insurance company data only; downloaded late February 2020.

[9] Please see the Annex A for methodology.

[10] E.g. rating requirements or capital requirements for investee companies.

[11] Limits are prescribed in percentage form in regulations.

[12] Some jurisdictions prescribe different limits for different types of pension funds (or among their sub-funds) and insurance companies (life insurance vis-à-vis general insurance). In such cases, pension funds and insurance companies were classified into categories provided in the relevant national regulation and were assigned the corresponding limits. This approach permits a more granular estimate. Actors were classified on best effort basis.

[13] Based on Preqin data on infrastructure investments through unlisted fund of direct participation.

[14] Under risk based regimes, allocation targets by investors may vary depending on riskiness of the assets they invest in. The different sizes and investment processes of investors imply that certain investors might have greater access to low-risk projects (domestically as well as abroad) and/or ability to manage such risks. This may lead to certain investors setting higher targets for infrastructure allocation than may be possible for other similar investors from the same country. The methodology presented herein ignores this distinction largely due to the unavailability of requisite data.

[5] Based on Preqin data on infrastructure investments through unlisted fund of direct participation.

[16] Certain jurisdictions prescribe different limits for different kinds of pension funds (or among their sub-funds) and insurance companies (life insurance vis-à-vis general insurance). In such cases, pension funds/ insurance companies were classified into categories provided in the relevant national regulation and

corresponding limits were taken. This approach permits a more granular estimate. Actors were classified on best effort basis.

[17] Based on Preqin data on infrastructure investments through unlisted fund of direct participation.

[18] Based on Preqin data on infrastructure investments through unlisted fund of direct participation

2 Assessing institutional investment in infrastructure

Accelerating and shifting institutional investment in green infrastructure requires a clear and granular understanding of the current investment landscape. This chapter presents a comprehensive empirical mapping of infrastructure investment by institutional investors domiciled in OECD and G20 countries with a view to assess progress and provide a baseline for future tracking. Currently, institutional investors hold USD 1.04 trillion worth of infrastructure assets. USD 314 billion of these are identified as investments in green infrastructure. For asset owners, the bulk of their infrastructure investment occurs through unlisted funds and project-level equity or debt, suggesting an illiquidity preference. Asset managers predominantly use securitised products for their infrastructure allocations. Investors exhibit a preference towards assets located within their region of domicile. For cross-border holdings, which are relatively limited, the lion's share is directed towards mature markets. This highlights the critical role of a domestic policy frameworks and an investment-grade enabling environment to attract and scale-up institutional investment.

An overview of how much is invested, through which financial instruments, and in which sectors, is an essential starting point for the discussion on how to accelerate and shift investment in new green infrastructure assets (OECD, 2018[1]). Granular data allows a targeted examination of how different types of institutional investors invest, or could invest, in infrastructure (as defined in Box 2.1). It is also fundamental to identify investment instruments and policy levers that can be used to transition to greener alternatives at the pace and scale needed.

This chapter presents results of an empirical mapping of current[1] infrastructure holdings by institutional investors domiciled in OECD and G20 countries. For the purposes of this report, the term *institutional investor* includes pension funds, insurance companies, sovereign wealth funds[2] and asset managers.

The quantitative mapping undertaken for this report contributes to wider efforts to plug investment information gaps. To that end, the empirical analysis below makes best efforts to overcome current data gaps. It should be noted that data unavailability on certain parameters, most notably bond ownership, use of proceeds and by extension structured debt products, continues to be a constraint. In the event more data becomes available, the estimates presented here may be revised retroactively, e.g. on the online data explorer accompanying the report or in possible future iterations of this empirical exercise.

This chapter begins with a brief overview of the underlying methodology for the mapping (details can be found in Annex 2.A), followed by a presentation of key findings and their implications. Building on the detailed presentation of data in this chapter, Chapter 3 discusses pathways and levers to scale-up green infrastructure investment.

Data on infrastructure investment

Data for the mapping exercise is sourced from multiple commercial databases. Commercial data is supplemented by primary data[3] collection and econometric techniques to fill gaps. The main databases used for data gathering are Thomson-Reuters (2020[2]), Preqin (2020[3]) and IJGlobal (2019[4]). The aggregation avoids double-counting and other overlaps by collecting data at a disaggregated level, at which distinctions are easily made, and then aggregating to the level presented here. For details on data treatment, the merging of databases as well as statistical and econometric techniques used to fill data gaps, see Annex 2.A.

The main results of the quantitative mapping are presented as Sankey charts. These charts provide a snapshot of current infrastructure investment by institutional investors. In other words, the charts below provide information on the current stock of investments, i.e. infrastructure holdings, and should not be misread as flows (i.e. time series data). At the core this exercise has the ambition to develop a baseline and inform the development of a forward view on how to shift and expedite the flow of institutional capital to support global climate and development objectives.

Box 2.1. Defining infrastructure

Broadly defined, infrastructure refers to the "[...] system of public works in a country, state or region, including roads, utility lines and public buildings" (OECD, 2020[5]). This also includes electricity transmission and generation assets. In investment parlance, investable infrastructure refers to self-liquidating physical assets, i.e. assets "paying for themselves" over time. The analysis in this report is guided by these definitions, with an emphasis on including sectors and types of physical assets commonly understood as infrastructure by the financial sector. Therefore hospitals, prisons etc., despite being buildings, are included as social infrastructure.

Real estate, such as commercial and residential buildings, is beyond the purview of the report as it is a separate asset class. Real estate investments merit a separate analysis, not least due to the contribution of commercial and residential buildings to global emissions. It must however be noted that infrastructure may be held through Real Estate Investment Trusts (REITs). REITs with infrastructure assets in their underlying portfolio (i.e. REITs that hold only infrastructure and no real estate) are included in the empirical mapping undertaken for this report. Further, nature-based infrastructure like ecosystem services like water filtration from catchment areas are excluded here as well. For a detailed list of which sectors are included in the analysis and how existing classifications in the underlying commercial databases are merged, see Annex 2.C.

In the case of listed securities, the report only includes stocks of companies with infrastructure operation and/or provision as a core part of their business model. Consequently, sectors that are normally included in publicly marketed infrastructure indices are included.

However, some financial assets through which institutional investors can hold infrastructure are often not linked to the properties of the underlying physical asset. For example, an infrastructure fund may hold non-infrastructure assets, e.g. non-infrastructure stocks. In the literature this distinction is commonly made and recognised as the basis for a debate on fake infrastructure (see box 2.2). To avoid counting fake infrastructure, non-infrastructure assets are manually removed in the mapping from indirect holdings e.g. through listed infrastructure funds.

Source: https://stats.oecd.org/glossary/detail.asp?ID=4511

Box 2.2.Is listed infrastructure really infrastructure?

Infrastructure assets are commonly used to diversify portfolios. Infrastructure generally offers predictable, inflation-linked cash flows and a low correlation to other assets making them attractive candidates to mitigate portfolio volatility. Such assets also provide long-term income and are suitable for investors with long-term investment horizons. At the core of infrastructure investments is their cash flow. However, the illiquidity of physical assets narrows the set of investors interested in these investments. Increasingly, the financial sector has seen a proliferation of listed infrastructure products, for instance infrastructure funds, which aim to combine the investment characteristics of infrastructure assets with liquidity.

Literature, however, suggests that many of the products marketed as listed infrastructure do not provide the investment characteristics and benefits of traditional infrastructure investing. For instance, in contrast to the expectation that a financial product linked to infrastructure would deliver a low correlation to other assets, an EDHEC analysis describes how infrastructure funds often highly correlate with market indices of listed assets in other sectors, and also often contain assets unrelated to infrastructure. The evidence shows that many of the analysed listed infrastructure funds do not serve as the hedging instrument they are expected or implied to be. Aside from these funds' inability to provide portfolio diversification, they also are as volatile as the listed stock market in general. Although they have the advantage of greater liquidity than most unlisted investments, these listed infrastructure fund investments are often not low-risk, stable or inflation-linked.

In light of considerations and concerns related to listed infrastructure products, this report includes investments from listed infrastructure funds (and listed infrastructure investments more broadly) only if they match the definition outlined in box 2.1. With this narrow inclusion, the analysis avoids misidentifying investment amounts and including investments that go beyond the scope of the report.

Source: https://edhec.infrastructure.institute/wp-content/uploads/2018/08/fakeinfra_EDHEC2017.pdf

The empirical mapping also includes, separately from other infrastructure investments, institutional investment in shares (*stocks*) of companies engaged in infrastructure development and/or operation. These securities of companies deriving revenues from infrastructure development, management and/or operation are often considered *listed infrastructure*. It is important to note, however, that stock prices of such corporations are determined by factors beyond the cash flow from physical assets, for instance market contagion. Further, investing in corporate stocks through secondary markets does not channel capital to the investee company[4]. As a result, an investment in an infrastructure-related corporate's stock has limited effect on new asset creation[5], which is the main focus of this report. Accordingly, direct stock holdings are presented and treated separately (see Figure 2.2).

As previously mentioned, unavailability of ownership and use-of-proceeds data for bonds is a constraint for the empirical mapping. Given the over-the-counter[6] (OTC) nature of the bond market, information available in commercial databases on the amount of investment made through corporate and other bonds is limited. The empirical mapping undertaken for this report therefore includes limited information on bond investments. Though it is difficult to precisely estimate the amount of institutional capital channelled towards new asset creation through corporate bonds (balance sheet financing), it should be noted that 80-90% of project-level debt finance is provided by commercial banks rather than institutional investors. In-depth interviews conducted for this report confirm this view. Therefore, while bonds play a role in institutional investment in infrastructure, given the prevalence of project finance and the focus of this report on new assets, missing bond information likely does not greatly reduce the comprehensiveness of the mapping exercise. Nonetheless, in the event more information is available, results presented hereafter may be updated retroactively in future iterations of this report and accompanying online sources.

Figures 2.1-2.14 illustrate sectoral splits, debt/equity preference, alignment with environmental goals and geographical splits. The taxonomy of investment channels is based on OECD (2015[6]). The figures aim to present comparable values (see Annex 2.A on comparability) and to provide, collectively, a composite picture of institutional investment in infrastructure.

Reading the Sankey charts

From left to right, the following Sankey charts track the origin and destination of institutional investment in infrastructure. Nodes on the far left show the sources of investment, categorised by type of institutional investor, while nodes on the far right show the final destination of capital by sector. Figures 2.1-2.4 show investment in seven broad sectors, while the Sankey charts following those drill down to the sub-sectoral level. It is important to note that information regarding assets invested in by certain infrastructure funds is unavailable. The amount allocated to such assets is ascribed to the category 'unknown' and excluded from all sectoral figures. For definitions of activities included in each sector, please refer to Annex 2.B. In the interest of readability, the Sankey charts do not differentiate between investment in physical assets and corporations.

Nodes located between the far left and far right present financial instruments through which investment is channelled. Except in the case of direct equity and debt, the ownership relation between the assets (grouped by sectors on the far right) and the investors (far left) is indirect. It is an analytical construction to highlight the diversity of the investment landscape. In other words, investment in assets should be read as *attributed to* rather than *made by* the investors. Depending on the financial instrument used, investors may be economic owners of the assets, legal owners or both. For instance, investors of unlisted funds[7] (*limited partners*) are economic owners of the fund's assets but not owners on record. All attributions in this report are made to reflect economic ownership. Annex 2.A covers details of this attribution and underlying estimation.

Box 2.3. Infrastructure investment strategies

Investment strategies of unlisted infrastructure funds can be categorised along the lines of the four categories widely used for real estate funds: *Core, Core Plus, Value-Add* and *Opportunistic*. They primarily indicate the relationship between risk and return of investments made by a fund. While distinctions between the strategies are relatively clear in real estate, strategies may overlap in infrastructure, and often *Debt* funds are considered an additional separate strategy.

A *Core* strategy is the least risky strategy, geared towards stable cash flow. Investments made under this category are typically held as alternatives to bonds. *Core* is comparable to what for listed equity markets would be called *income*.

A *Core Plus* strategy is a strategy with low to moderate risk, geared towards increasing cash flows and allowing for some lack of predictability. In infrastructure, an example would be a well-utilised asset that is in need of major maintenance during the time horizon of the investment. **Core Plus** is comparable to what for listed equity markets would be called *growth and income*.

A *Value-Add* strategy is a strategy with moderate to high risk, geared towards high cash flow once the infrastructure assets in question have been upgraded, or value has been added. *Value-Add* is comparable to what for listed equity markets would be called *growth*.

An *Opportunistic* strategy is the riskiest strategy. Typical examples would be greenfield projects or where an asset is repurposed. *Opportunistic* is comparable to what for listed equity markets would be called *growth*.

While the above strategies typically focus on equity investments, there are also distinct infrastructure funds with *Debt* strategies. Debt strategies in themselves can be diverse, ranging from less risky to highly risky debt products included in the fund. Debt funds can hold diverse products, making further categorisation difficult. Generally investors look for exposure to debt, and beyond that may have to discuss risk-preferences on a case-by-case basis with fund managers.

In addition, certain infrastructure funds may be involved in *secondary transactions*. This includes an unlisted fund purchasing infrastructure assets from another unlisted fund.

Source: https://pathwaycapital.com/wp-content/uploads/2019/08/Investing_in_Infrastructure.pdf

Figure 2.3 presents investment in green infrastructure only. Given the absence of a globally accepted definition of green infrastructure, this report undertakes a comparative analysis of select sustainable finance taxonomies, green bond definitions and guidelines from OECD and G20 countries (see Annex 2.B for details and methodology). The objective of the comparative exercise is to identify the lowest common denominator in terms of sectors accepted across all analysed sources to be green. Certain sectors are unequivocally considered green, for instance solar or wind, while certain others are unequivocally not, for example fossil fuels. However, there are infrastructure sectors for which climate and other environmental implications are not quite as clear, for instance roads. For the purpose of this analysis only the sectors accepted as green by all or most of the reference sources considered are included. Figure 2.3 reflects this. It must be noted that according to some reference sources, certain sectors are considered green only if the assets meet a prescribed emission or other threshold. The absence of asset-level emission data makes it difficult to apply this conditionality to the dataset. For the purpose of analysis in this report, therefore, relevant assets are deemed to meet the prescribed thresholds. In other words, the investment amount ascribed to green assets in this report presents an upper bound or the most optimistic attribution.

Findings from the empirical mapping

Overview charts and green investments

Figures 2.1 and 2.2 together provide a snapshot of the current institutional holdings in infrastructure - a total of USD 3.34 trillion. As shown in Figure 2.1, USD 1.04 trillion is allocated through all instruments (other than listed stocks). Unlisted funds are the dominant conduit of these infrastructure investments, with USD 380 billion (ca. 37%) in invested assets. USD 173 billion is currently held in direct project equity, with USD 26 billion in direct project debt. Investment through securitised structures including REITS, YieldCos[8], MLPs and INVITS[9] together represent 43% of current institutional investment. As shown separately in Figure 2.2., ca. USD 2.3 trillion is directly held in listed stocks of companies developing, managing and/or operating infrastructure assets (listed infrastructure). As discussed above, as stock investments do not channel capital to the investee company and therefore cannot direct capital to new investments, the remaining analysis, including in Chapter 3, does not take these investments into account.

Figure 2.3 presents current holdings of institutional investment in **green** infrastructure, which in total amounts to USD 314 billion. This equals 30% of all institutional investment in infrastructure (excluding investment in corporate stocks). Approximately 49% of all investment in green infrastructure is channelled through YieldCos (USD 155 billion). Unlisted funds and direct project equity follow YieldCos, with USD 93 billion and USD 44 billion, respectively. It is important to note that while unlisted funds account for 37% of investment in Figure 2.1, only 31% of their capital is currently allocated to green assets. This suggests that there is considerable potential upscale green infrastructure investment through unlisted funds. To contrast, 97% of all investment held through YieldCos is allocated to green infrastructure.

Figure 2.1. Institutional investment in infrastructure (excl. direct investment in stocks) - USD 1.04 trillion

Holdings of institutional investors domiciled in OECD and G20 countries (as on February 2020)

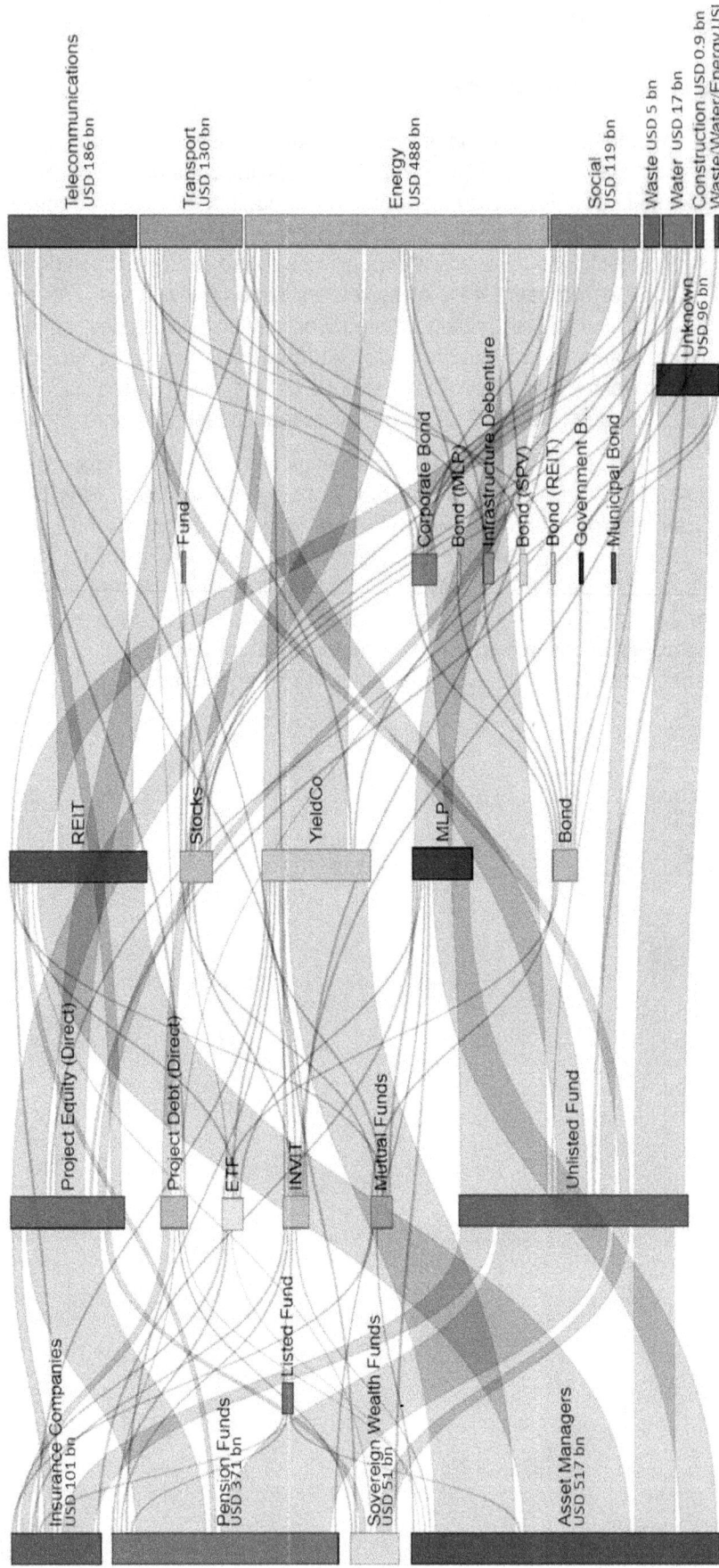

Note: The figure excludes direct stock holdings (see Figure 2.2, which includes direct stock holdings only). Further, while some nodes appear to have unequal left and right sides, this is just a visual effect and they are always balanced.

Source: Authors

Figure 2.2. Institutional investment in infrastructure -related corporate stocks - USD 2.3 trillion

Holdings of institutional investors domiciled in OECD and G20 countries (as of February 2020)

Note: Though some nodes appear to have unequal left and right sides, this is just a visual effect and they are always balanced.
Source: Author

Figure 2.3. Institutional investment in green infrastructure (excl. direct investment in stocks) - USD 314 billion

Holdings of institutional investors domiciled in OECD and G20 countries (as on February 2020)

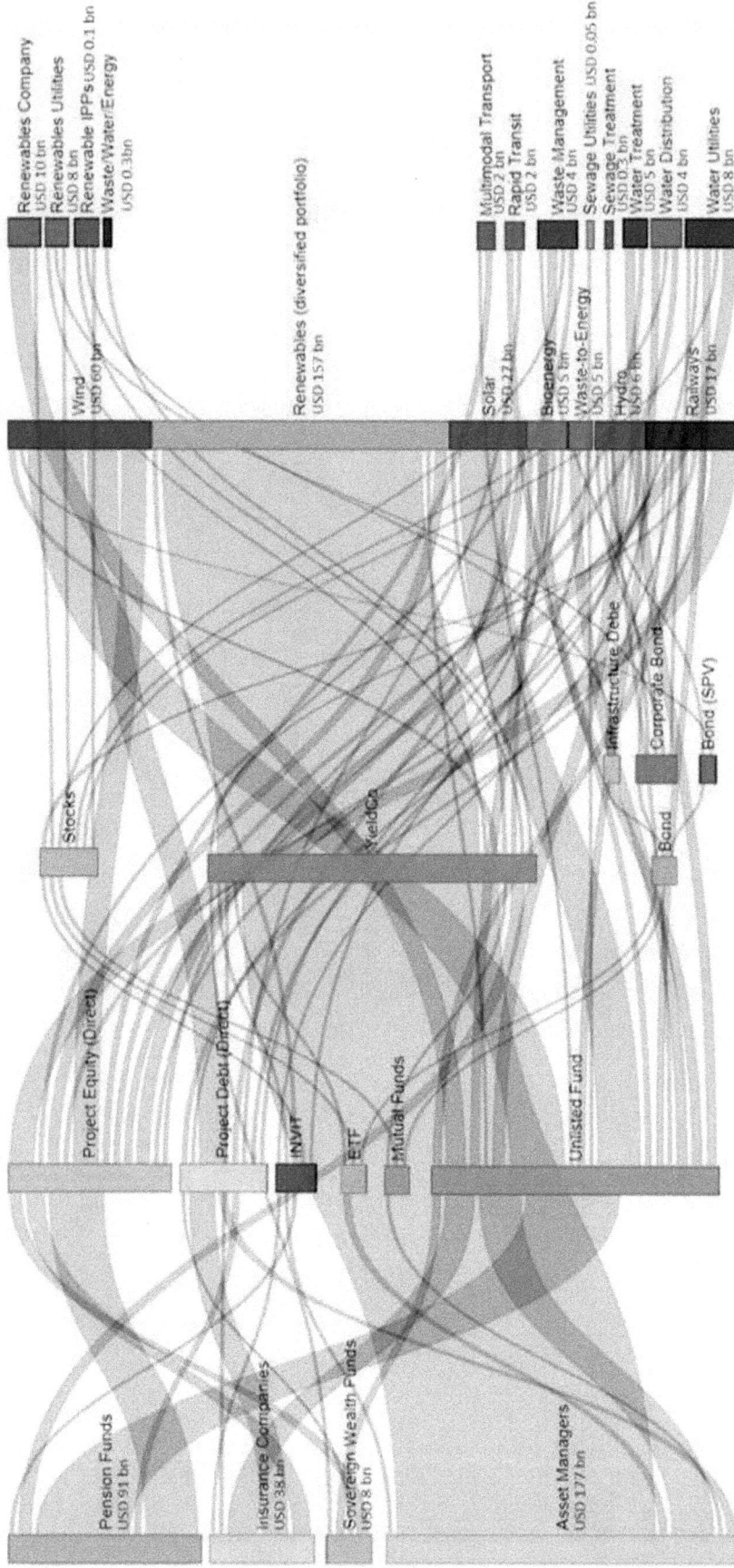

Note: The figure excludes direct stock holdings. Further, while some nodes appear to have unequal left and right sides, this is just a visual effect and they are always balanced.
Source: Authors

The exposures provided by the variety of instruments can be broadly characterised either as exposure to financial assets or exposure to real assets (the latter having stronger linkages to the real economy). The most direct exposures to real assets are provided by direct investment at the project level, unlisted funds and securitised structures like YieldCos, INVITs and REITs.

Figure 2.3 narrows the mapping to the present holdings of institutional investment in green infrastructure. The role of direct investments, unlisted funds and securitisation is even more pronounced in the investment landscape for green infrastructure assets, where they account for almost all investments. In the context of accelerating and shifting institutional capital towards green infrastructure, these three instruments merit further investigation. Chapter 3 focuses on direct investment, unlisted funds and securitised vehicles and discusses the potential of these instruments for scalability.

In terms of origin of investment, it is essential to recognise differences between asset owners (pension funds, insurance companies and sovereign wealth funds) and asset managers. Activities of asset owners and managers are driven by different considerations and different incentives.

Pension Funds

Among asset owners, pension funds account for over 71% of the investment depicted in Figure 2.1 (i.e. excluding investments in listed corporations). Over 90% of these pension fund investments are made through direct equity and unlisted funds, in comparison to small holdings in YieldCos and INVITs. These allocations suggest long-term capital appreciation as a major driver of infrastructure investment, and an illiquidity preference possibly incentivised by the illiquidity premium. Data on pension fund commitments in unlisted funds shows a shift in recent years towards riskier strategies, e.g. value added (see Box 1.3 above for a categorisation and explanation of strategies). This is line with the overall market drift towards riskier infrastructure strategies (UBS, 2019[7]). Increasing risk appetite of pension funds is unsurprising given persistent low yields on traditional assets: Non-core strategies provide comparatively high returns and greater opportunities for capital appreciation. One implication of this trend going forward is potential increment in institutional capital available for construction stage projects.

Of the USD 371 billion currently invested by pension funds in infrastructure, 25% is allocated to green assets. A closer look at transaction data reveals that annual direct equity investment by pension funds in 'non-green'[10] assets consistently exceeds that in green. This is driven by investment in natural resources infrastructure and in buildings (social infrastructure such as hospitals). The lack of emission data for all buildings included in the mapping, makes it difficult to distinguish the share of green buildings. However, given that only a small share of the global stock of buildings is green, it is safe to consider the amount directed towards buildings as investment in non-green assets. On the debt side, the lion's share of direct debt is extended to renewable energy projects. Debt investment in fossil fuel projects stood at 50% of the debt extended to renewables in 2019 (mainly by private pension funds).

The bulk (75%) of infrastructure investment by pension funds is channelled through unlisted funds. Based on capital committed in funds with vintages[11] after 2010 and taking a fund lifespan of 15 years, at least USD 40 billion[12] can be considered unavailable for shifting to greener investments. This demonstrates the importance of the choices made and instruments used by long-term investors. The illiquidity and financial lock-in of their investments in non-green infrastructure leads to lock-in of higher emissions and a delayed opportunity to shift to green infrastructure. Disaggregation to the regional level in section on cross-regional investments below provides further insights into the investment behaviour of pension funds.

Insurance Companies

In contrast to pension funds, insurance companies appear to have relatively modest investment holdings in infrastructure. This is explained by different investment preferences of life and general insurers. Infrastructure allocations are primarily made by life insurers on account of their long-term liabilities. General insurers typically underwrite infrastructure instead of investing long-term given their need for short-term liquidity. The infrastructure holdings mapped for this report therefore include investment by life insurers and represent a subset of total insurance assets in OECD and G20 countries. At USD 101 billion in infrastructure assets, investment by insurance companies is ca. 10% of all infrastructure investment. Like pension funds, insurance companies' infrastructure investment also appears to be guided by long-term capital appreciation—with 81% of current investment established through unlisted funds and direct equity provision. About 38% of total insurance company investment is allocated to green assets. Direct equity investment by insurance companies in green assets has been on a steady upward trajectory in recent years, chiefly due to investments in wind and solar projects. In 2018, direct debt investment by insurance companies in renewables far exceeded that in fossil fuels (Preqin, 2020[3]). In 2019 however, the data shows a reversal i.e. a higher share of direct debt provision to fossil fuel projects. Commitments by insurance companies in unlisted funds with vintages[13] after 2010 suggest at least USD 12.5 billion[14] locked in non-green assets (versus USD 6 billion in green assets).

Sovereign Wealth Funds

Sovereign wealth funds (SWFs) appear to play a limited role in the infrastructure investment landscape. The absence of disclosure around portfolios of SWFs may be one explanatory factor. A second factor is that, in OECD and G20 countries, SWFs have significantly less combined AUM (USD 3.6 trillion) than e.g. pension funds (USD 33 trillion), in part simply because not every country has an SWF. Based on the current mapping, SWFs (like pension funds and insurance companies) seem to invest in infrastructure assets for long-term capital appreciation and possibly illiquidity premium. The share of SWF investment in non-green assets through unlisted funds has been increasing in recent years--driven by investment in fossil fuel projects and natural resources infrastructure. Green investment through unlisted funds is led by wind and solar. There is a recent trend of countries creating SWFs to mobilise capital towards specific policy objectives. SWFs of this nature may be capitalised by national Governments as well as SWFs of other countries, as in the case of NIIF in India. Strictly speaking such SWFs have a different nature than commercial financial entities and are better placed within the context of public sector de-risking.

Asset Managers

Listed instruments dominate infrastructure investment by asset managers. Read together, Figures 2.1 and 2.2 show that over 90% of infrastructure investment, i.e. ca. USD 2.4 trillion, by asset managers is allocated to stocks (USD 2 trillion). This is followed by units of YieldCos (USD 153 billion), MLPs (USD 71 billion), mutual funds (USD 5.1 billion), ETFs (USD 3.5 billion), REITS (USD 201 billion) and INVITS (USD 2 billion). Besides the asset owners covered in this report (pension funds, insurance companies and SWFs), asset managers invest on behalf of an array of other clients as well (e.g. retail investors). These other clients, unlike asset owners, have a low illiquidity tolerance and risk appetite. Stocks and units of securitised vehicles offer the benefits of liquidity and stable distributions. Apart from stocks and units of securitised vehicles, asset managers invest ca. USD 77 billion through unlisted funds – this excludes equity participation (as a limited partner) by asset managers in their own funds (funds where the asset manager is the general partner).

Asset managers hold ca. 56% of total institutional investor holdings of green infrastructure (Figure 2.3). This is largely due to investment in YieldCos, which account for 49% of institutional investment in green infrastructure and are a major investment conduit for renewables investment. The value of YieldCos is driven, at least in part, by factors other than the underlying assets, for instance market contagion. Therefore, this major vehicle for institutional investment in green infrastructure can be considered to have significant but not exclusive exposure to underlying infrastructure assets.

Other Instruments

Direct infrastructure debt comprises a small portion of the investment landscape. Compared to equity, infrastructure debt is a relatively new asset type for institutional investors. Underlying investment data exhibits a rising interest in infrastructure debt in recent years, both through direct transactions as well as commitments to funds pursuing an infrastructure debt strategy. With persistently low yields on corporate and sovereign bonds, infrastructure debt presents an attractive fixed-income alternative to institutional investors. Government and investment-grade bond yields are expected to be further compressed in the aftermath of the COVID-19 pandemic-- infrastructure debt stands to profit from this trend. In-depth interviews conducted for this report support this view. Among the direct debt transactions tracked for this report, investment in green assets far exceeds that in non-green assets. This is driven by debt extended to renewable energy projects. In terms of asset owners, insurance companies are the most active in this space.

As mentioned previously, data on bond ownership is opaque. Bond investment tracked in Figure 2.1 amounts to USD 0.5 billion. This value must be read as a lower bound of institutional infrastructure investment through bonds in light of data limitations. With this caveat in mind, a look at the sectors invested in, reveals a diverse use of bonds. Bonds can be an effective instrument to raise capital for infrastructure from investors looking for predictable income-generating assets - this includes investor types other than institutional. Some jurisdictions have bond products dedicated to infrastructure, for instance infrastructure debentures in Brazil and infrastructure bonds in India. Based on discussions with experts, green bonds and other labelled fixed-income products have to date not delivered significant financing for infrastructure projects. The most direct means are through green project bonds but that to date has accounted for only a small fraction of the market.

As Figure 2.1 further shows, institutional infrastructure investment channelled through exchange-traded funds (ETFs)[15] and mutual funds dedicated to infrastructure amount to USD 2.7 billion and USD 5.2 billion, respectively. Note that these numbers must be read as lower bounds as well. Ownership data for ETFs and mutual funds is often incomplete, thereby preventing the mapping from including institutional investments through funds with uncertain and unknown ownership.

Investment in physical asset versus corporate

As shown in Figure 2.4, the lion's share of the investment through unlisted funds and direct equity and debt is directed towards physical assets. 22% of the money channelled through unlisted funds is allocated to unknown sources, and 7% is allocated to corporates. These include renewable energy IPPs, private companies that operate and/or manage infrastructure.

Figure 2.4. Investment in physical asset vs. corporates through unlisted funds and direct investment

Source: Authors

Primary versus secondary stage investment

Most of the current positions through unlisted funds and direct project-level equity investment are established through secondary stage investment, i.e. acquisition of operational projects (Figure 2.5). Risk profile of projects is the most elevated during construction phase. However, once projects are operational, project risk is lowered and becomes more palatable to institutional investors. While this preference for operational projects is a longstanding trend, primary stage investment activity by institutional investors has increased in recent years, as in-depth interviews confirm. Construction stage projects with their higher risk-adjusted returns offer an attractive avenue to investors searching for higher yields. As exhibited in Figure 2.5 below, the share of direct debt investment allocated to primary stage opportunities almost equals debt extended to secondary stage projects. Declining yields in the bond market and rising risk appetite of institutional investors (as evidenced above) augur well for increased construction stage credit provision by institutional investors.

Figure 2.5. Primary vs. secondary stage investment through unlisted funds and direct investment

Source: Authors

Sectoral breakdowns

A more granular look at the sectoral level provides additional insights into the current investment landscape. Figures 2.6-2.12 show the different sectors and differences in instruments used between sectors. Like in figures 2.1 and 2.3, corporate stocks are excluded.

Energy

Figure 2.6 shows an overview of institutional investment in energy infrastructure. Of all infrastructure sectors, energy accounts for the largest investment holdings with USD 488 billion. Asset managers hold energy assets worth USD 263 billion, USD 159 billion is held by pension funds, USD 48 billion by insurance companies and USD 18 billion by SWFs.

Notably, the largest sub-sector in institutional energy holdings (excluding listed stocks) is renewables. For more information, see the breakdown of renewables investments in Figure 2.7. Since much of fossil fuel-based energy infrastructure is held by corporations, much of the institutional investment in this sub-sector is held through shares of these corporations (see Figure 2.2).

Other than renewables, Figure 2.6 shows investment in fossil fuel-based energy infrastructure. Fossil fuel-based energy infrastructure includes, among others, coal, gas, oil power plants, heating as well as natural resource infrastructure (for instance pipelines and storage facilities for oil and gas). Further, smaller categories are nuclear energy and energy efficiency[16]. The utilities sub-category consists mostly of power utilities that could not be categorised further due to lack of data.

A look at the instruments reveals the centrality of YieldCos, but also highlights the role of MLPs particularly for the natural resources infrastructure. Note that the energy sector is the only sector in which MLPs are used, as fossil-based energy projects are the only eligible projects. With USD 73 billion, MLPs account for 15% of institutional investment in fossil fuel based infrastructure. Notwithstanding the currently exclusive association between MLPs and fossil fuel based infrastructure, the potential of the MLP structure to channel large sums of capital towards real assets (physical assets) is noteworthy. The role of securitised vehicles in scaling-up investment in green infrastructure is discussed in Chapter 3.

Figure 2.7 shows a breakdown of institutional investment in renewable energy infrastructure. Diversified renewables portfolios are the largest category at USD 157 billion, followed by wind (USD 60 billion) and solar (USD 27 billion). Almost all investment in diversified renewable portfolios is held through YieldCos. Lack of data regarding fair values of constituent assets prevents splitting the renewables portfolio category further. However, details (in quarterly reports of YieldCos) regarding installed capacity of portfolios indicate that most of the underlying assets are wind and solar power plants.

As figures 2.1 and 2.2 show, stocks and YieldCos constitute the bulk of total investment by asset managers in infrastructure. As mentioned previously, asset managers invest on behalf of a variety of clients besides institutional investors (e.g. retail investors and high net-worth individuals). These clients have different risk-return preferences (e.g. lower tolerance for illiquidity), to which YieldCos are well-suited; they provide liquid access to physical assets like renewable energy projects. See Chapter 3 for more details.

Figure 2.6. Institutional investment in energy infrastructure (excl. direct investment in stocks) - USD 488 billion

Holdings of institutional investors domiciled in OECD and G20 countries (as on February 2020)

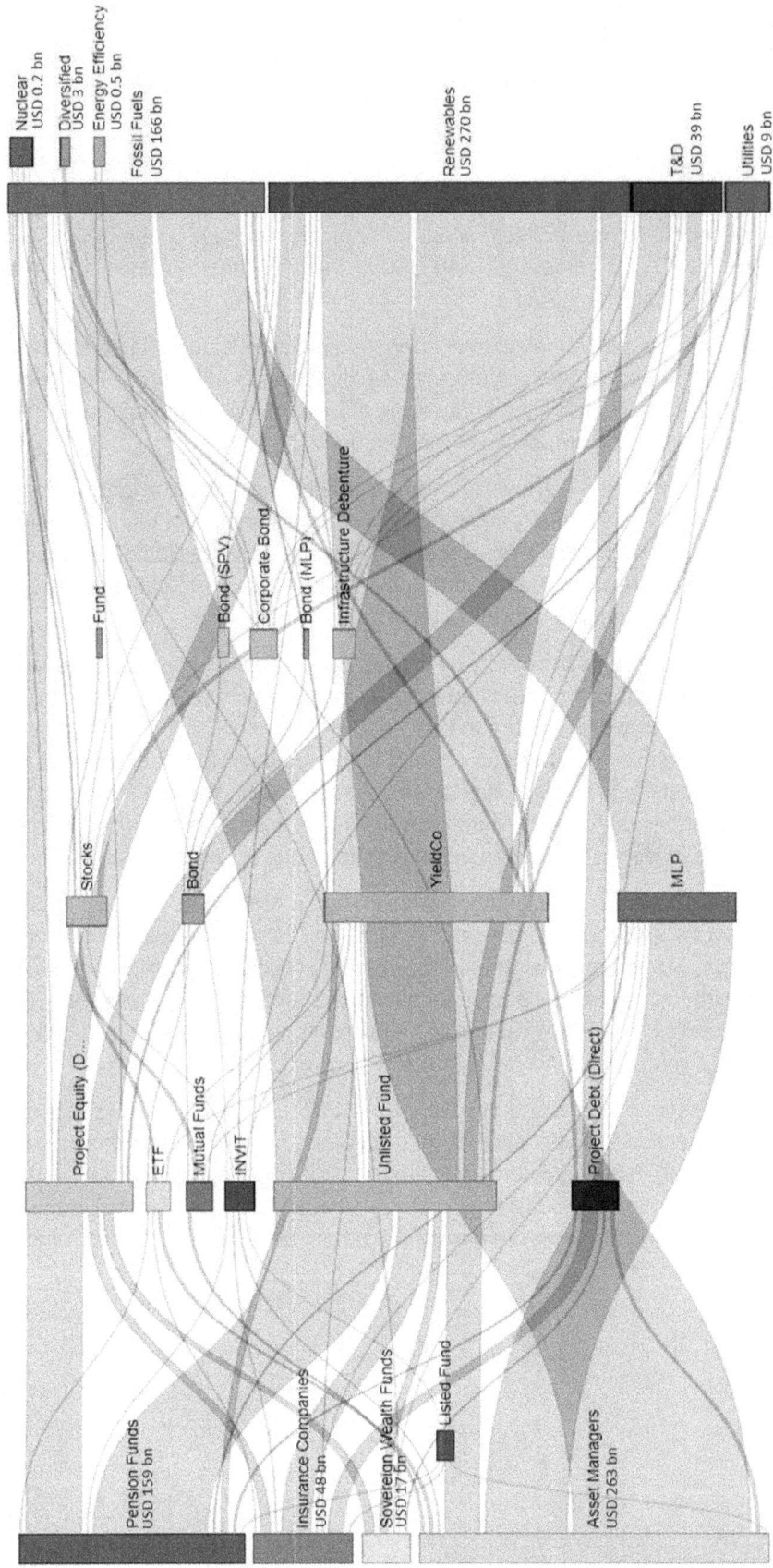

Nuclear
USD 0.2 bn

Diversified
USD 3 bn

Energy Efficiency
USD 0.5 bn

Fossil Fuels
USD 166 bn

Renewables
USD 270 bn

T&D
USD 39 bn

Utilities
USD 9 bn

Fund

Bond (SPV)

Corporate Bond

Bond (MLP)

Infrastructure Debenture

Stocks

Bond

YieldCo

MLP

Project Equity (D...

ETF

Mutual Funds

INVIT

Unlisted Fund

Project Debt (Direct)

Pension Funds
USD 159 bn

Insurance Companies
USD 48 bn

Sovereign Wealth Funds
USD 17 bn

Listed Fund

Asset Managers
USD 263 bn

Note: The figure excludes direct stock holdings. Further, while some nodes appear to have unequal left and right sides, this is just a visual effect and they are always balanced.

Source: Add the source here. If you do not need a source, please delete this line.

GREEN INFRASTRUCTURE IN THE DECADE FOR DELIVERY: ASSESSING INSTITUTIONAL INVESTMENT © OECD 2020

Figure 2.7. Institutional investment in renewables (excl. direct investment in stocks) -USD 278 billion

Holdings of institutional investors domiciled in OECD and G20 countries (as on February 2020)

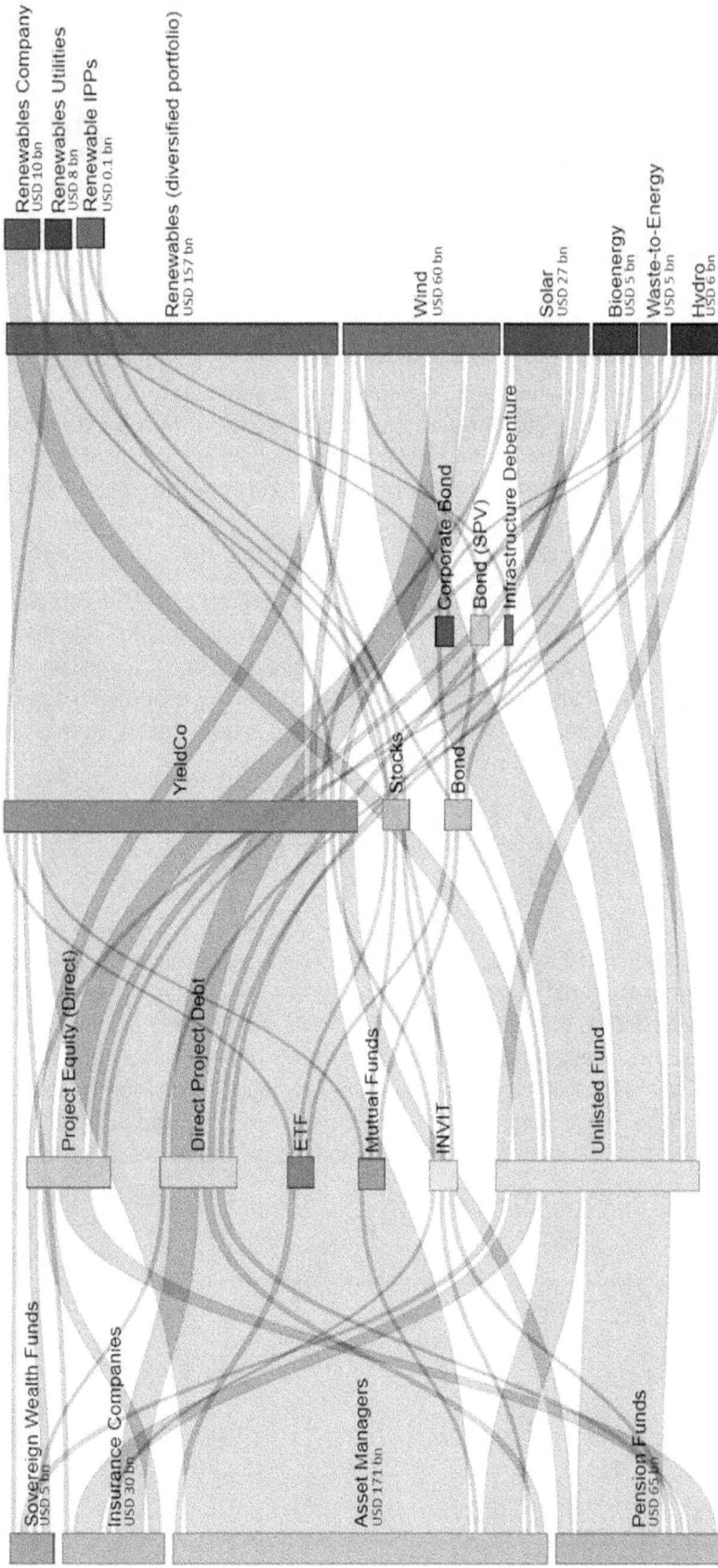

Note: The figure excludes direct stock holdings. Further, while some nodes appear to have unequal left and right sides, this is just a visual effect and they are always balanced.
Source: Add the source here. If you do not need a source, please delete this line.

GREEN INFRASTRUCTURE IN THE DECADE FOR DELIVERY: ASSESSING INSTITUTIONAL INVESTMENT © OECD 2020

Transport

Figure 2.8 shows the breakdown of institutional investment in infrastructure (USD 130 billion). Of the total amount tracked, only 16% (USD 21 billion) is presently allocated to green infrastructure. The largest single sub-sector is roads with USD 42 billion. Roads (which include toll roads, bridges, tunnels and highways), airports, ports etc. are core infrastructure assets. Such assets generally offer steady revenue streams, often through concessions or availability payments[17]. Well-established project finance structures exist for transport infrastructure in most jurisdictions analysed in this report. This can be seen in the role of direct project equity and unlisted funds, which are used for ca. 45% and ca. 47% of total transportation infrastructure investment, respectively.

Transport infrastructure provides essential services. Historically, revenues from transport Infrastructure have been stable, as revenues from concessions or availability payments are generally predictable, following broader economic activity trends. However, they may not be immune to large economic shocks. Assets with merchant risk[18] can be particularly susceptible to demand shocks such as the one caused by the COVID-19 public health emergency. The demand shock resulting from pandemic-control shutdown measures caused some investors to devalue some transport assets in their portfolios, notably shares of airport operators. To shore-up the attractiveness of critical and green infrastructure like rapid transit systems, proposals have been made to implement public de-risking measures covering revenue shortfall during such exceptional demand shocks.

The use of securitised products for transport infrastructure is relatively modest compared to the energy and telecommunications sectors. However, INVITs are a noteworthy recent addition to the transport investment landscape. Investment through INVITs already stand at USD 1.5 billion i.e. around a third compared to more establish securitised vehicles like REITs (USD 4.6 billion). This is driven by a rising interest in monetising operational assets, both by the public and private sector, to free construction stage equity in certain markets (for instance India).

The prevalence of pension funds is unsurprising given the alignment between their long-dated liabilities and the long-term predictable revenues from transport assets.

Telecommunications

Figure 2.9 shows the breakdown of institutional investment in telecommunications infrastructure (USD 186 billion in total). Asset managers hold the largest share among institutional investors (USD 139 billion) primarily through REITs (ca. 96%). Wireless communication infrastructure including telecom towers is the largest recipient of institutional investment. Telecom towers have been relatively unaffected by the COVID-19 crisis. Going forward, the sector is expected to see higher capital allocation by institutional investors. Internet-related infrastructure (fibre optic cables, data centres etc.) is also expected to receive higher institutional investment on the back of expected demand growth and resilience exhibited during the pandemic (Infrastructure Investor, 2020[8]).

Figure 2.8. Institutional investment in transport infrastructure (excl. direct investment in stocks) - USD 130 billion

Holdings of institutional investors domiciled in OECD and G20 countries (as on February 2020)

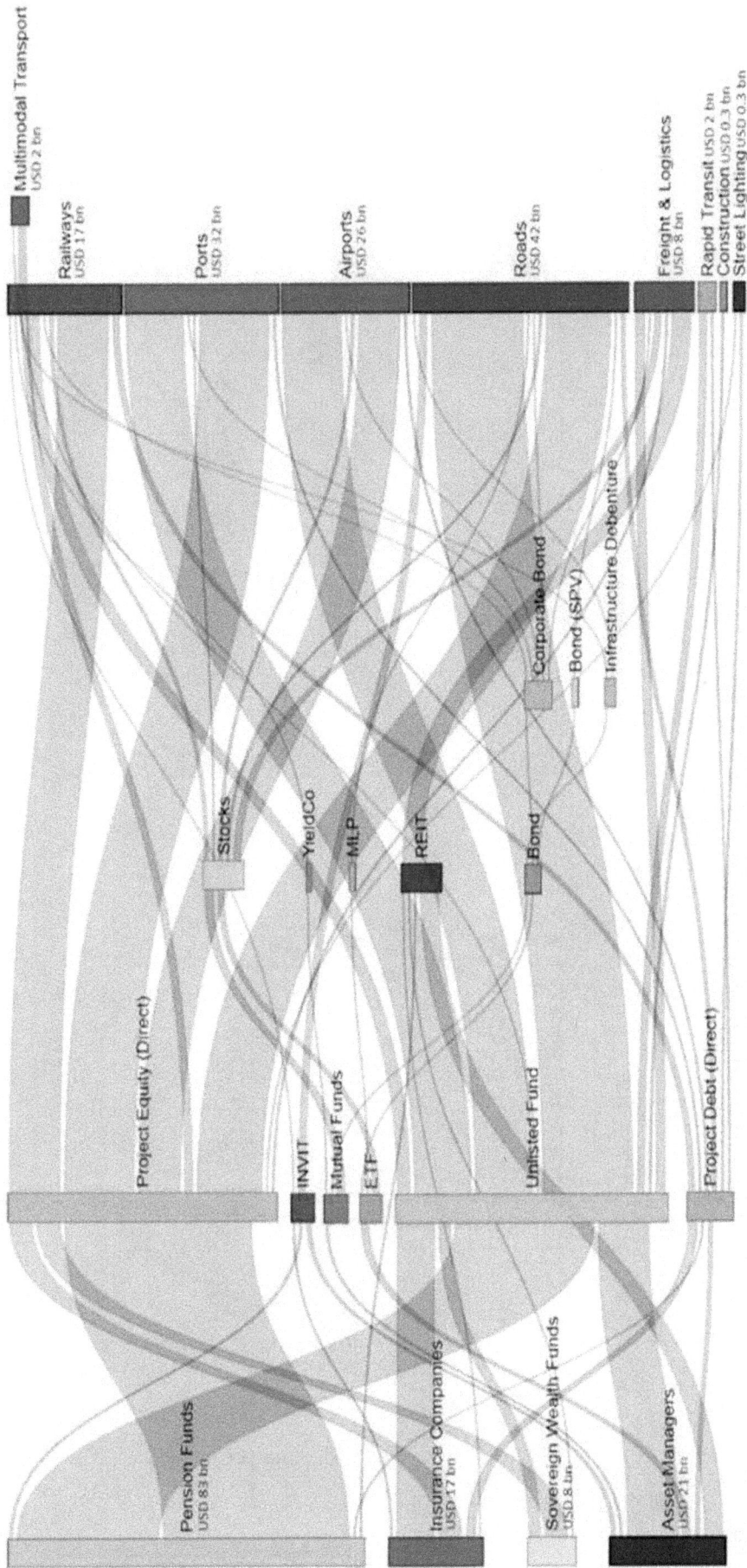

Note: The figure excludes direct stock holdings. Further, while some nodes appear to have unequal left and right sides, this is just a visual effect and they are always balanced.
Source:

GREEN INFRASTRUCTURE IN THE DECADE FOR DELIVERY: ASSESSING INSTITUTIONAL INVESTMENT © OECD 2020

Figure 2.9. Institutional investment in telecommunications infrastructure (excl. direct investment in stocks) - USD 186 billion

Holdings of institutional investors domiciled in OECD and G20 countries (as on February 2020)

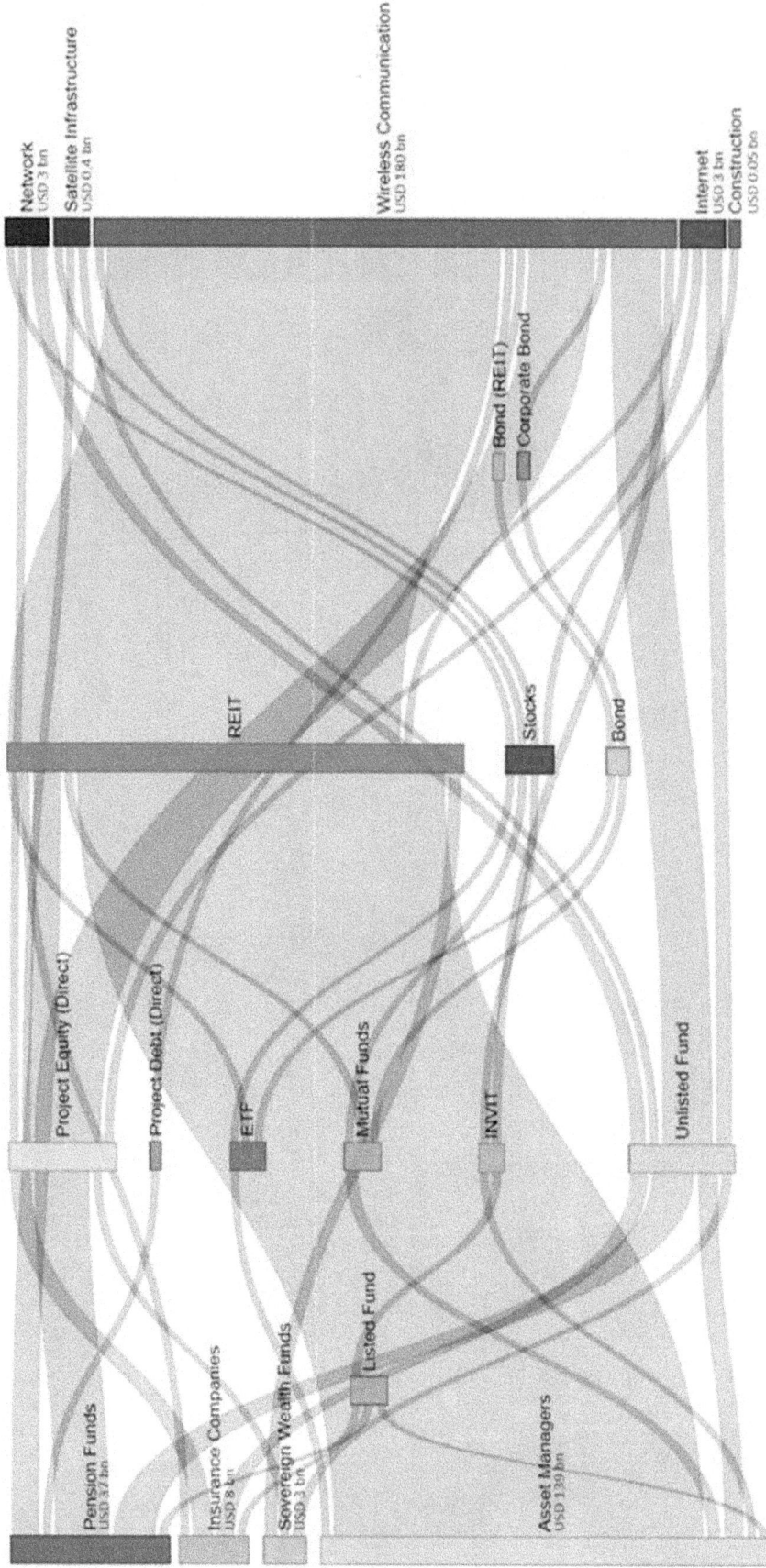

Note: The figure excludes direct stock holdings. Further, while some nodes appear to have unequal left and right sides, this is just a visual effect and they are always balanced!
Source: Authors

Figure 2.10. Institutional investment in social infrastructure (excl. direct investment in stocks) - USD 115 billion

Holdings of institutional investors domiciled in OECD and G20 countries (as on February 2020)

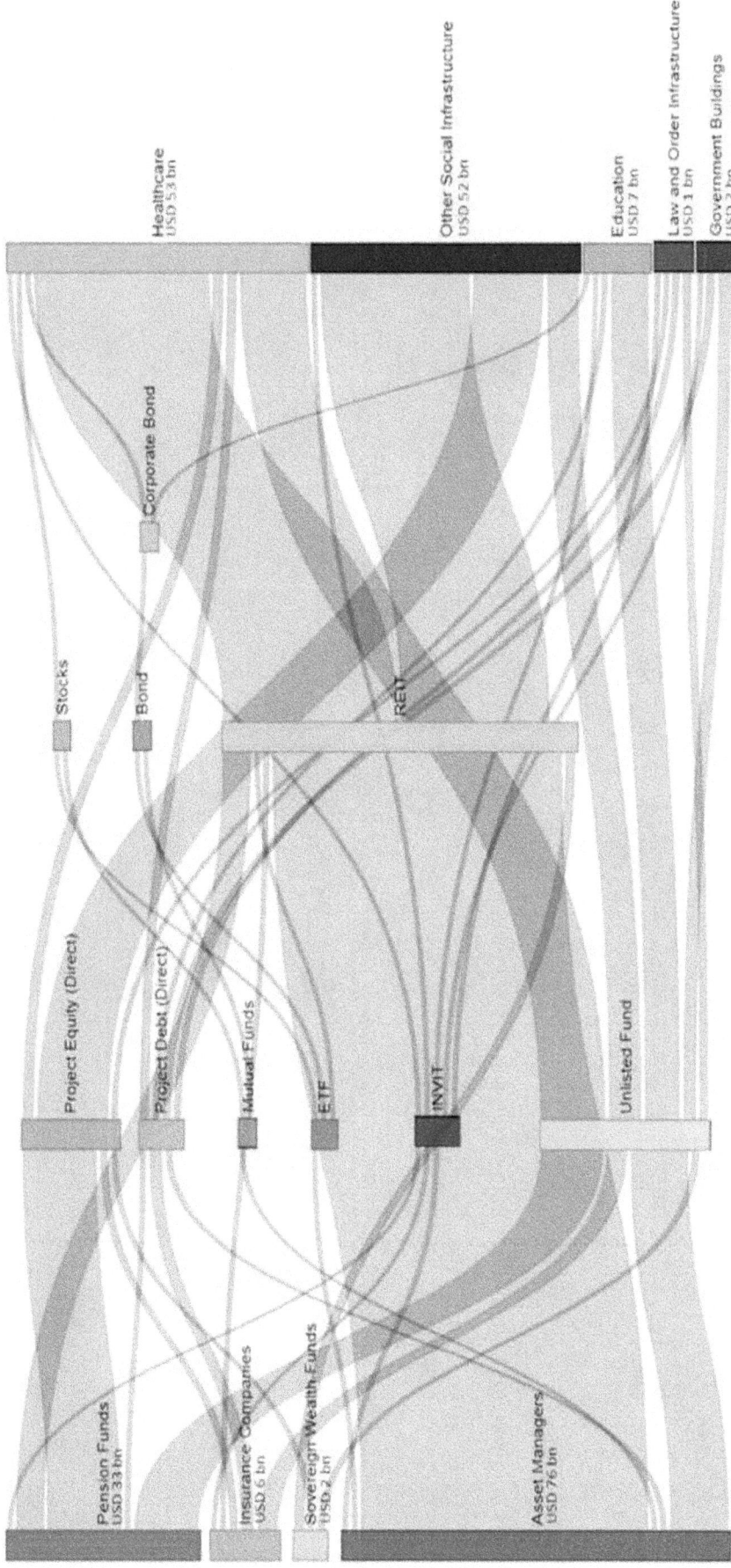

Note: The figure excludes direct stock holdings. Further, while some nodes appear to have unequal left and right sides, this is just a visual effect and they are always balanced.
Source: Authors

Figure 2.11. Institutional investment in water supply infrastructure (excl. direct investment in stocks) - USD 17 billion

Holdings of institutional investors domiciled in OECD and G20 countries (as on February 2020)

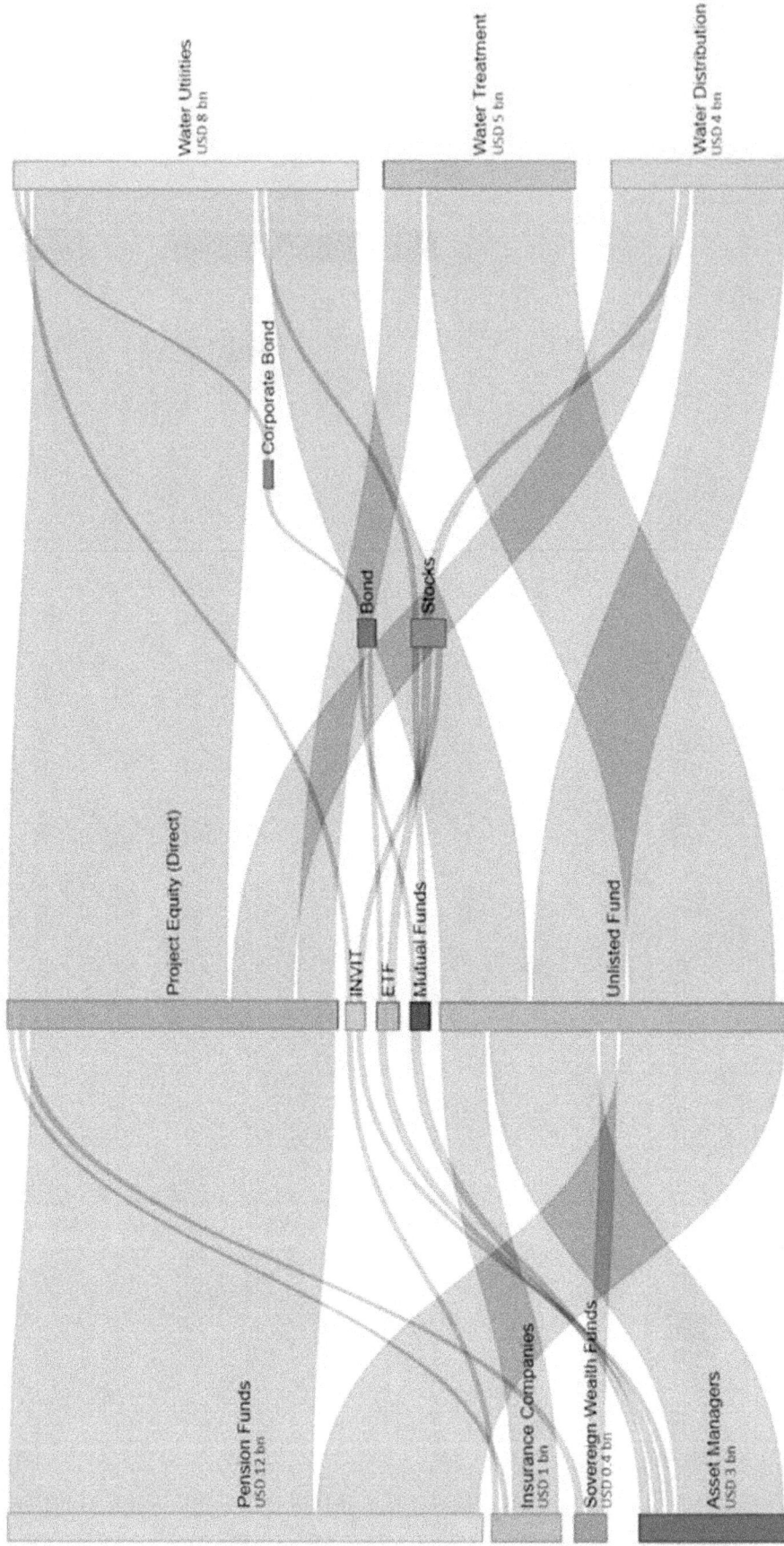

Note: The figure excludes direct stock holdings. Further, while some nodes appear to have unequal left and right sides, this is just a visual effect and they are always balanced.

Source: Authors

Figure 2.12. Institutional investment in waste management infrastructure (excl. direct investment in stocks) - USD 4 billion

Institutional Investors domiciled in OECD and G20 countries (as on February 2020)

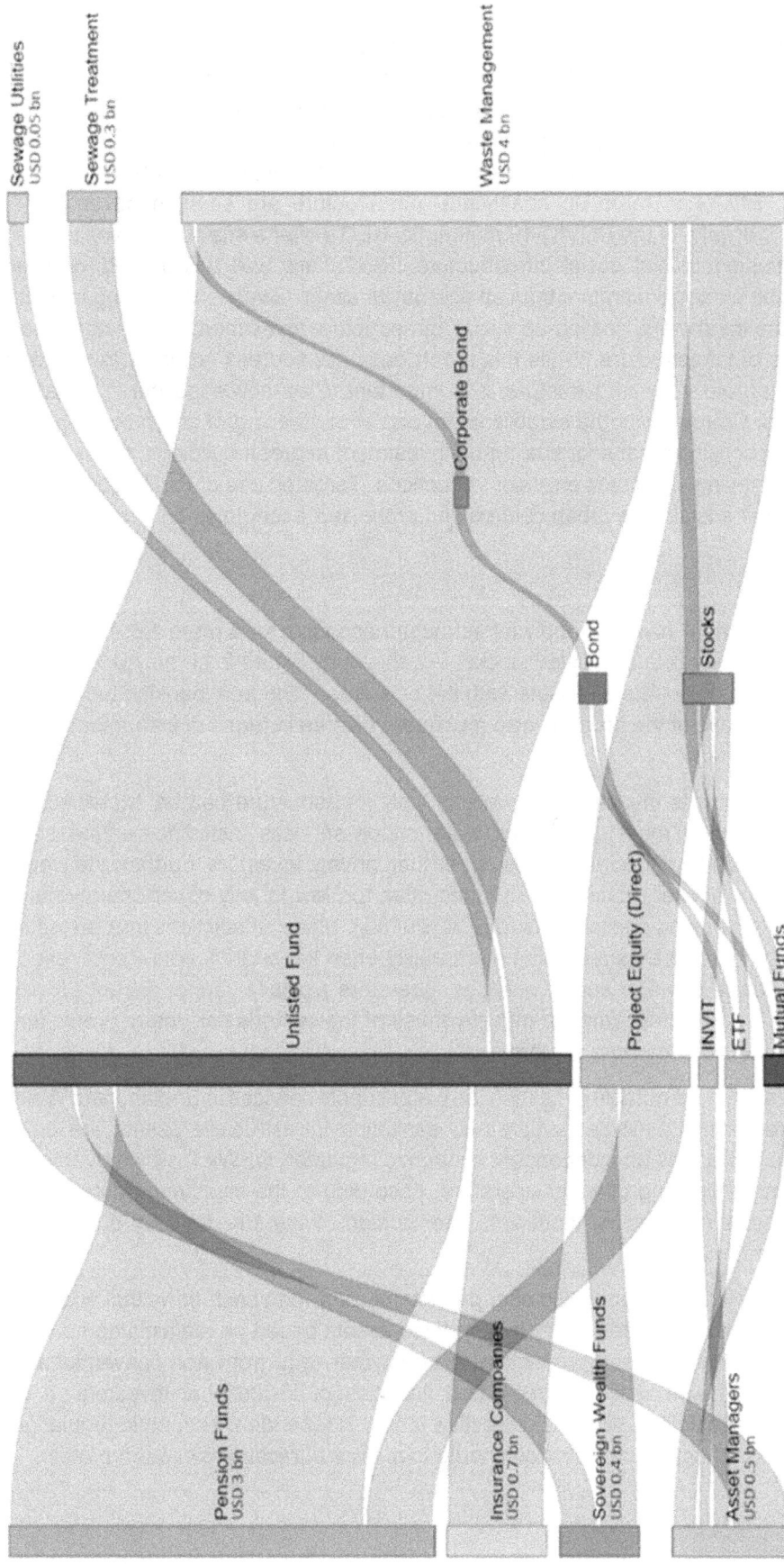

Note: The figure excludes direct stock holdings. Further, while some nodes appear to have unequal left and right sides, this is just a visual effect and they are always balanced.

Source: Authors

GREEN INFRASTRUCTURE IN THE DECADE FOR DELIVERY: ASSESSING INSTITUTIONAL INVESTMENT © OECD 2020

Social infrastructure

The lion's share of investment in social infrastructure is channelled through unlisted funds and REITs. As shown by Figure 2.10, REITs and unlisted funds account for 84% of total investment. Healthcare is the largest sub-sector at USD 53 billion, i.e. 46% of all institutional investment in social infrastructure. Given that social infrastructure mostly comprises of buildings, the use of REITs is unsurprising. The need for healthcare, education and other social assets is critical to deliver on global climate and development commitments. Efforts to ramp up healthcare infrastructure are seen in government spending plans announced in the wake of the COVID-19 pandemic. REITs offer a scalable means to channel more capital towards developing crucial social infrastructure. REITs are well established vehicles and are often considered to be a traditional rather than an alternative asset. Given longstanding industry experience and comfort with the instrument, scaling-up social infrastructure investment is, in a certain sense, easier than for other kinds of infrastructure. While this report does not address green buildings, as real estate is an asset class separate from infrastructure, it is important to acknowledge the important role of REITs for green buildings. Coupled with the establishment and strengthening of green building codes, targeted use of REITs is a promising means for scaling-up investment in green buildings, delivering sustainable urban centres and achieving significant emission reductions. Targeted use of REITs coupled with green building codes can deliver sustainable urban centres and propel our economies on a low-emissions trajectory.

Water supply infrastructure

Institutional investment in water supply infrastructure accounts for a mere 1.6% of all investment holdings mapped in this report (excluding listed stocks). As shown by Figure 2.11, only USD 17 billion[19] is presently invested in water supply -related assets, with the bulk emanating from pension funds (USD 12 billion). The investment landscape of the sector is also much less diverse in terms of instruments and vehicles used to channel private capital.

Modest levels of private investment in water supply infrastructure can be explained by some structural aspects of the sector. In most jurisdictions, water supply services, including treatment and distribution, are owned and financed by public authorities rather than private investors. Further, the water sector generally has a poor record of cost recovery, with tariffs often too low to fully cover operational and maintenance costs, and rarely covering capital costs (OECD, 2018[9]). Many jurisdictions lack an independent regulator for tariff setting and concerns regarding affordability often keep tariffs below cost reflective levels. Given the essential nature of water supply services, operators typically cannot disrupt services in the case of non-payment. These factors limit the attractiveness of the sector's risk-return profile for private investors compared to other infrastructure sectors.

The UK water sector is a notable exception, as water supply services in England and Wales were privatised in 1989 (Ofwat, 2020[10]). Water supply and sanitation infrastructure assets are privately owned and managed. The sector has an independent economic regulator, OFWAT, which oversees tariff setting and capital investment planning of water operators. According to the investment data tracked for this report, 56% of the assets included in figure 2.11 are located in the UK, held by domestic and international institutional investors.

In principle, water infrastructure could offer predictable long-term cash-flows that align well with long-dated liabilities. Steady revenues derived from long-lived assets based on inelastic demand, such as for water supply services, treatment and production of bulk water (e.g. from non-conventional sources, such as desalination), align well with the long-dated liabilities of institutional investors. A stronger enabling environment for investment, with cost-reflective tariffs, independent economic regulation and ring-fenced revenue streams for operators would contribute to a more attractive risk-return profile .

Waste management infrastructure

Figure 2.12 shows that institutional investors invest in waste-related and circular economy infrastructure mainly through unlisted funds, with 87% (USD 4 billion) of their holdings through this instrument. Waste-related infrastructure mostly consists of waste management infrastructure which contains sub-categories such as infrastructure for circular economy, and cannot with the current data be disaggregated into smaller categories. Other categories are sewage treatment and sewage utilities[20]. They are both exclusively held through unlisted funds. While this finding may be a result of the small number of investments, it may also reflect a need for special expertise. Unlisted funds may be more likely to acquire the expertise necessary for these types of investment than other instruments

Cross-regional investments

Figures 2.13-2.16 below present cross border holdings by institutional investors from OECD and G20 countries, categorised by region of the investor's domicile. The Figure exhibits cross border investment in real assets through unlisted funds, direct equity and debt as well as INVITs where participation in the initial set-up and placement of the vehicle is known. Investment holdings through REITs YieldCos and MLPs are excluded due to lack of clarity on which positions were established during the initial placement and which positions were established through the secondary market. This distinction is observed given this report's focus on the real economy impact of institutional investment.

Each pair of chord diagrams in Figures 2.13-2.16 presents outbound investment (to all regions including the investor's region of domicile) in all infrastructure and green infrastructure (i.e. a subset of all infrastructure). With the exception of investors from the Middle East and Europe, institutional investors allocate the majority of their capital to assets located in their region of domicile. This propensity is even stronger, and without exception, for green infrastructure investment—the lion's share of green infrastructure investment by institutional investors is channelled within their regions of domicile.

Among Asian investors, SWFs and insurance companies are most active in infrastructure investment, led by the Chinese SWF and insurance companies from South Korea. Among Asian pension funds, investment activity by South Korean pension funds far exceeds that by others in the region.

European pension funds are the most active investors in their region—led by funds from the United Kingdom, Netherlands and Denmark. Pension funds from the United Kingdom and Denmark also lead capital allocation to green infrastructure. Among insurance companies, German insurers hold the largest amount in green infrastructure assets, followed by companies from Denmark. In general, European institutional investors exhibit a preference towards mature markets.

52 |

Figure 2.13. Outbound investment by institutional investors (grouped by region of domicile)

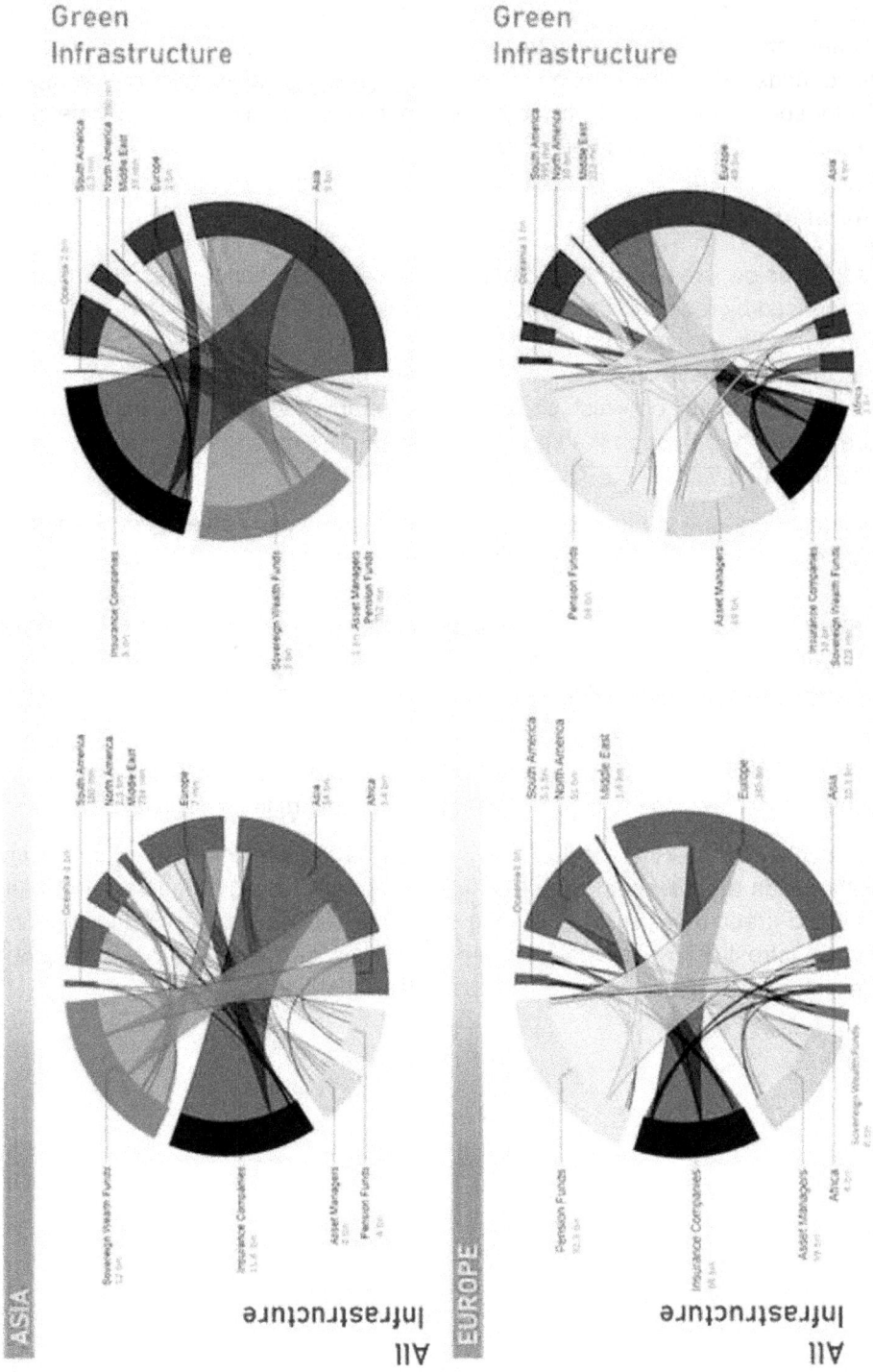

Source: Authors.

Figure 2.14. Outbound investment by institutional investors (grouped by region of domicile)

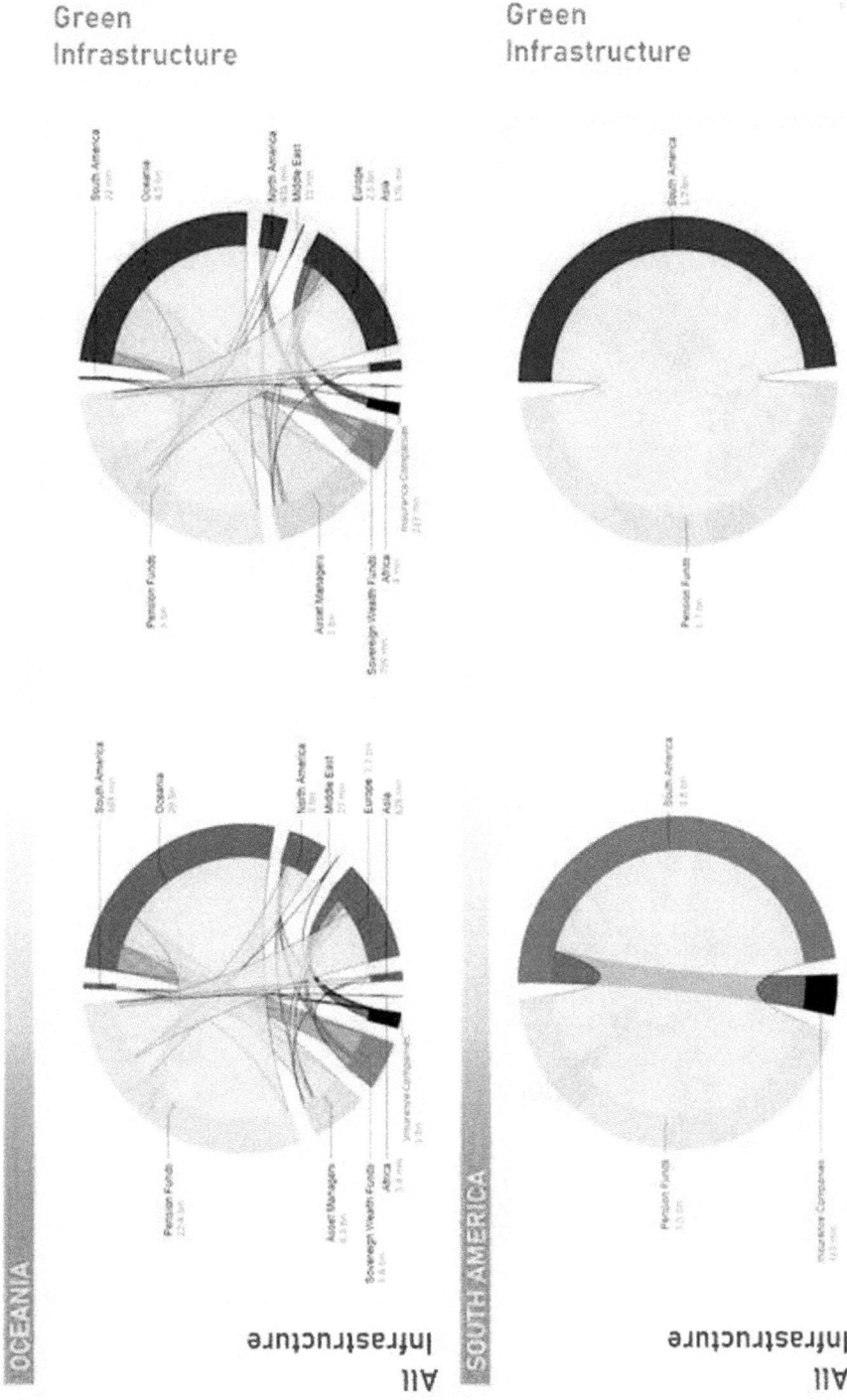

Source: Authors.

Figure 2.15. Outbound investment by institutional investors (grouped by region of domicile)

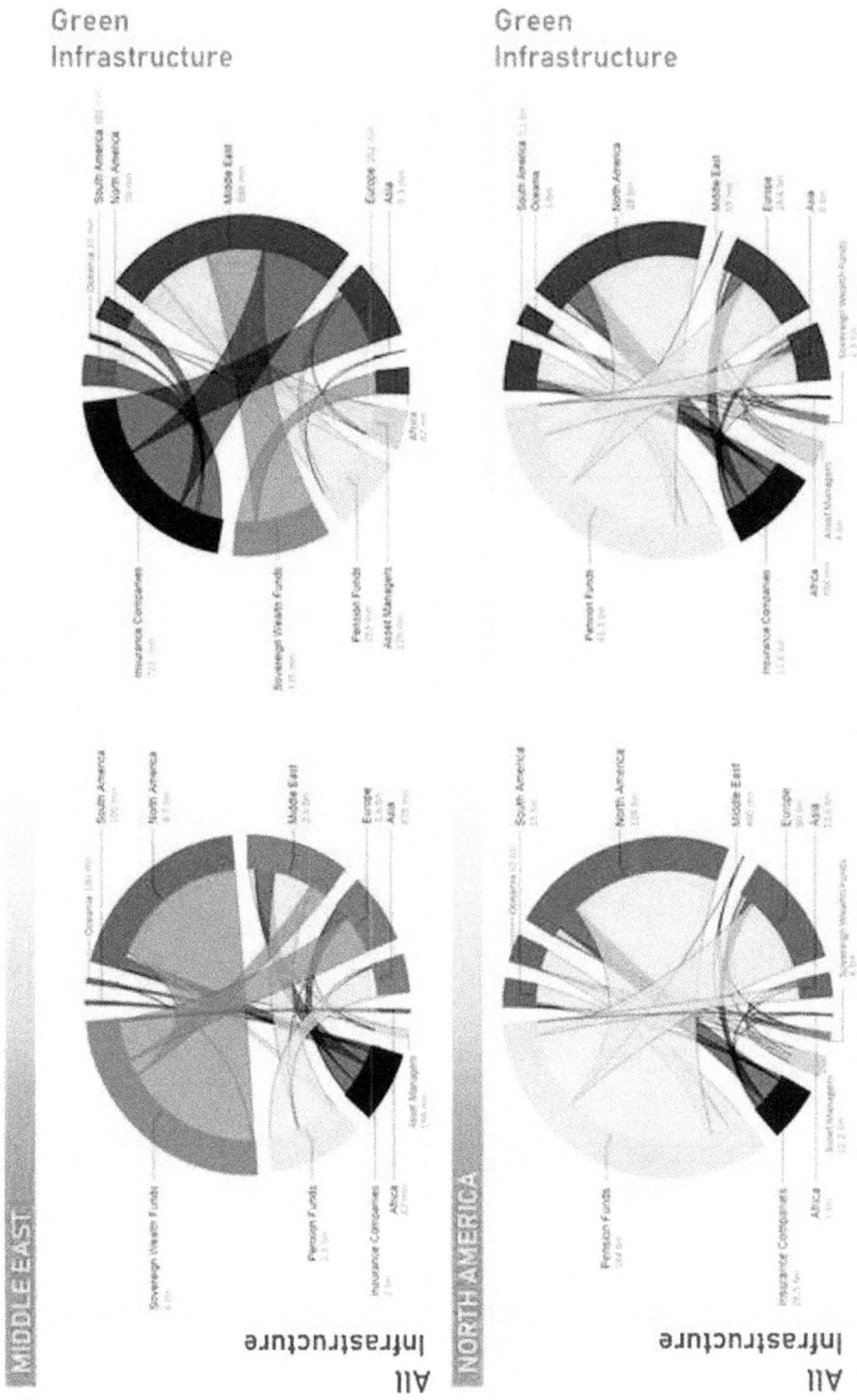

Figure 2.16. Outbound investment by institutional investors (grouped by region of domicile)

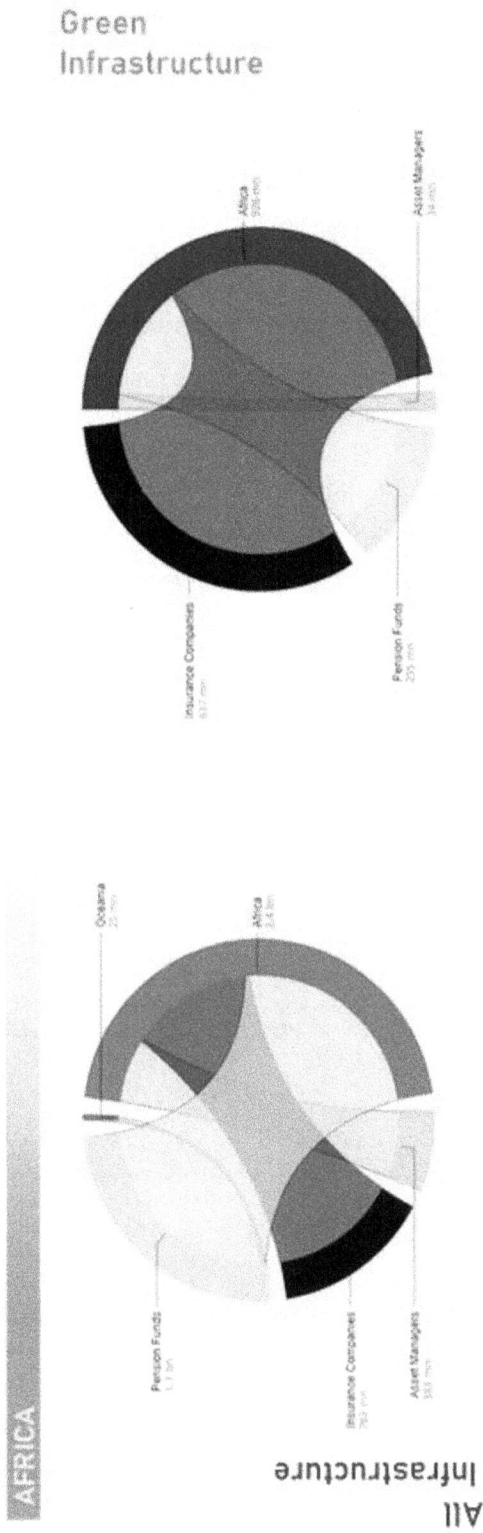

Source: Authors.

56 |

In Oceania, pension funds are the most active investors in infrastructure, followed by asset managers. Investors from the region also exhibit a preference towards assets located in mature markets.

South American investors demonstrate the strongest inward preference. Investment activity is led by Brazilian pension funds with all capital allocated to assets within South America.

Among institutional investors in the Middle East[21], SWFs have the highest amount allocated to infrastructure with a clear preference for assets located in mature markets. The entire amount is attributable to investment by the SWF of Saudi Arabia. This is followed by pension funds and insurance companies from Israel. Insurance companies domiciled in Israel lead the region's investment in green infrastructure with bulk of the capital allocated to assets in Middle East and Europe.

Among North American investors, pension funds are the most active investors in infrastructure – led by pension funds from Canada. They are followed by insurance companies domiciled in the United States. North American investors also demonstrate a preference towards mature markets.

The chord diagram for Africa is comprised entirely of South African investors. Pension funds lead investment in infrastructure overall with a strong African preference. The majority of green infrastructure investment originates from insurance companies who also exhibit a domestic preference.

Figure 2.17 provides an overview of cross-border investment amounts.

Figure 2.17. Cross-border investment holdings (all) of OECD and G20 institutional investors

Through unlisted funds, direct investment and INVITs (USD Million)

ASSET REGION

INVESTOR REGION	Africa	Asia	Europe	Middle East	North America	Oceania	South America	**Total**
Africa	2,413					25		2,438
Asia	3,412	14,051	6,811	734	2,474	3,723	380	31,585
Europe	3,854	6,298	134,764	1,242	26,640	4,536	1,709	179,043
Middle East	87	880	1,632	2,475	4,674	130	101	9,978
North America	1,072	12,620	59,938	490	123,755	14,765	15,149	227,789
Oceania	6	628	7,659	27	2,920	19,939	369	31,548
South America							3,833	3,833
Total	10,844	34,477	210,805	4,967	160,463	43,118	21,541	486,215

Source: Authors

These findings on cross-border investments highlight that institutional capital exhibits a strong regional preference. The cross-border investments that do take place are primarily targeted at assets located in mature markets. This highlights the critical role of domestic policy frameworks and an investment-grade enabling environment to attract and scale-up institutional investment. Chapter 3 discusses this in greater detail.

Key takeaways

A persistent low yield environment is increasingly prompting institutional investors to look to alternatives to obtain higher returns. While infrastructure assets presently account for only a small portion of investable institutional AUM, they offer avenues for higher returns as well as income. Empirical mapping undertaken for this report suggests that infrastructure allocations of pension funds, insurance companies and SWFs are geared at long-term capital appreciation and opportunities to earn an illiquidity premium.

The mapping shows asset managers' preference for liquid assets. This highlights the potential of securitised structures such as YieldCos, INVITs and infrastructure REITs to scale-up real economy infrastructure investment. Of the institutional investors under study, asset managers have the largest holdings of green infrastructure assets owing to their investments in REITs and YieldCos.

Unlisted funds, direct project-level equity/debt and securitised products are important instruments to upscale green infrastructure investment. Further, data tracked[22] for this report points towards a rising risk appetite among investors, particularly pension funds, that bodes well for scaling-up primary stage investment going forward. Direct infrastructure debt is a growing asset type and can offer an attractive alternative to low yielding bonds as well as an increasing source of credit for new assets.

Institutional investors' choices of financial instruments for infrastructure investment can have important implications for the low-carbon transition. Money channelled towards non-green assets through instruments with low liquidity and lock-in periods, like unlisted funds, can lock-in long-term emissions.

Institutional investors demonstrate a preference towards assets located within their region of domicile. This propensity is more pronounced in case of green infrastructure. Data also shows a clear tendency of cross border investment majorly when assets are located in mature markets. This speaks to the importance of a conducive policy environment to attract and scale-up institutional investment in infrastructure.

While this report doesn't analyse in detail the impact of COVID-19 on the infrastructure sector, there are early signs that the pandemic might have accelerated an already changing paradigm vis-à-vis sectoral preferences. Coverage around industry sentiment and priorities suggest that telecommunication, in particular data centres and internet-related infrastructure, is poised to receive larger allocations. Another category that might receive increased investor attention is social infrastructure. REITs can be especially useful to scale-up capital allocation towards healthcare and education assets. Additionally, infrastructure spending will form an essential pillar in government efforts around the world to fuel economic activity. This stands to add to the momentum in the private sector and create an opportunity to build green infrastructure that can avoid long-term emission lock-in and ensure public health and wellbeing.

Annex 2.A. Methodology

Data for the Sankey charts in chapter 2 are the result of merging multiple databases containing infrastructure investment data. Merging these databases poses several definitional and technical challenges, most notably challenges regarding data gaps as well as diverging or overlapping definitions of actors and sectors. The following describes how the analysis underlying the Sankey charts of chapter 2 tackles these challenges.

All investment data used in this report derives from the infrastructure database of Preqin (2020[3]), the listed securities and listed funds EIKON database of Thomson-Reuters (Thomson-Reuters, 2020[2]) and the infrastructure deal database of IJGlobal (IJGlobal, 2019[4]). Note that despite the overlapping scopes of the above-mentioned databases, there is no overlap or double-counting in the aggregated data.

With the aim of comparability, Figures 2.1-2.XYZ were aggregated in a manner that accounts for differences in investment valuation. For example, while stock investment data is directly attributable to an investor, investments made through unlisted funds have to be attributed based on commitments to funds and based on information of these funds' asset deals.

Estimation methodology

Institutional investment data suffers from quality and availability gaps. Data gaps are mainly due to general lack of disclosure on the type of business transactions included in this report. Availability gaps may also be due to the data gathering processes of underlying commercial data. To provide a reasonable attribution and an aggregate picture of investments, these gaps must be plugged with estimations.

To develop a composite view of global infrastructure investments, this report employs statistical techniques to estimate investment values where gaps were found. Since the nature of data gaps differs between, and sometimes even within databases, estimation methods differ as well. The statistical techniques used for this report aim to leverage the provided information as effectively as possible to develop representative estimates.

Wherever possible, observed investment data is used. Any unobserved values are replaced through prediction-based approaches. When prediction is infeasible or does not lead to robust results, estimations rely on averaging over peer-groups of the observations in question. The following sections provide details on the prediction, averaging and aggregation methods employed and discusses how investment values are attributed to investors and sectors.

Unlisted funds

For investments made through unlisted funds, the estimated and observed data is used to construct an indirect ownership relationship between investors and infrastructure assets. Note that investors in a fund are not the owners on record of the invested assets and the returns for a fund's investor are based on the portfolio of the fund's underlying assets.

The bulk of the observations for unlisted funds are sourced from Preqin (2020[3]), containing open-ended and closed infrastructure funds, participating in relevant infrastructure transactions. In preparation for estimations, all past owners are excluded. This is to ensure that the aggregated results only reflect current investment.

The total commitments of institutional investors in all funds in the database amount to 3533. Of these, 1318 commitments are observed and 2215 commitments are estimated. The total number of all deals executed by unlisted funds in Preqin (2020[3]) and additional[23] transactions by relevant unlisted infrastructure funds added from IJGlobal (2019[4]) amounts to 1766. Of this, transaction amounts for 857 deals are observed and 909 are estimated.

Although individual deals cannot directly be attributed to the investors of a fund, investments of a fund can be attributed to investors of that fund according to how much the single investors committed to the funds in question.

Annex Figure 2.A.1. Estimation and attribution process for unlisted funds data

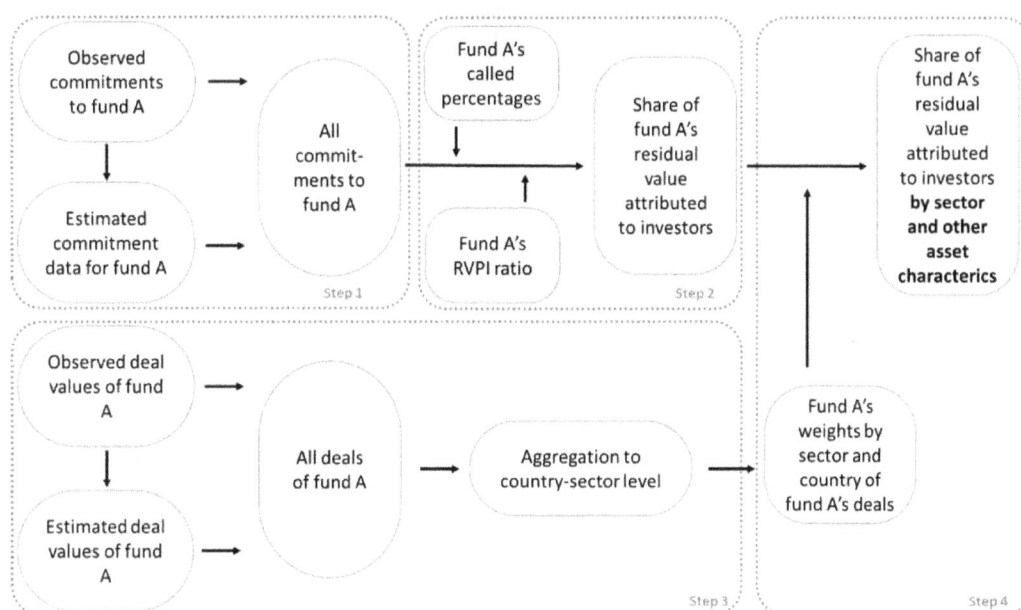

Note: Investment through funds captured in the IJGlobal (2019) database is added separately based on deal value only.
Source: Authors.

Figure 2A.1 shows the attribution of current fair value of an investor's investment through an unlisted fund based on that investor's commitment in the fund. Guided by the pro-rata distribution principle underpinning limited partnership structures, the commitment values can be used as weights of the fund's residual value to estimate the fair value of an investor's investment in that fund.

In line with this approach, in **step one** shown in Figure 2A.1, all unobserved commitment values are estimated using econometric techniques. Following the pro-rata distribution principle, based on the called[24] percentage information and the RVPI[25] (residual value to paid-in), **step two** calculates the residual value-equivalent of an investor's commitments.

A similar approach is employed for the transactions side to construct an indirect ownership relationship. To do so, unobserved values of transactions by all observed infrastructure funds are estimated in **step three**. Deal values are used as weights and applied to the residual value of the fund to calculate the sectorial allocation of the fund in **step four**. This means that the deal value based weights are also applied to the fair value of an investor's investment to develop an investor-sector-region observation.

Note that direct attribution of several commitments to sectors is impossible since data on the fund that links them is missing. Instead, the calculation assumes that the average shares found for the commitments that can be attributed is representative for the commitments with missing fund data as well. The calculation therefore attributes the residual value-equivalents according to these average sector shares in commitments of the rest of the sample.

The econometric technique used to estimate and predict unobserved values is described in the following paragraphs. Figure 2A.2 presents an overview of the hierarchy of estimation methodology followed to ensure a consistent use of the best method applicable. For the definition of sectors and merging of sector-definitions, see Annex 2.B.

Annex Figure 2.A.2. Hierarchy of Methodology followed

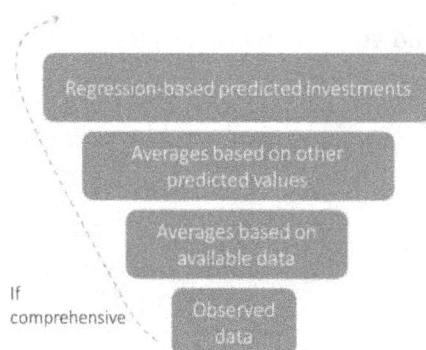

Source: Authors.

Commitment values estimated in step one above, are based on information on the fund, its AUM[26] and its investors. Based on these regression results, predicted values are filled in where no commitment value is observed. The adjusted R^2 of 0.89 confirms that the model is well adjusted. An F-test confirms the significance of the model as a whole. A Breusch-Pagan test confirms absence of heteroscedasticity and comparing Akaike information criterion values confirms the choice of the model over alternatives that were run as robustness checks. Further, comparisons of in-sample predictions with observed values show that even outlying values are never more than twice the observed value, pointing towards reasonable accuracy of the predictions.

In cases where an out of sample prediction of commitments is not possible due to missing data, the missing commitment values are replaced by averaged commitment values. Averages are calculated on the closest peer-group of observed commitments, and if data is missing, averages are calculated based on a less directly comparable peer-group. The closest peer group for calculated commitment averages is a group of commitments with the same industry, strategy, country and inception year of the fund. These categories are gradually relaxed to less comparable peer-groups if missing data could not be filled in.

Deal values estimated in step three depend on available information about the deal as well as asset information, as well as information on the fund investing in the deal[27]. Based on regression results, predicted values are filled in where no deal value is observed. The adjusted R^2 of 0.75 confirms that the model is well adjusted. As for the commitment regression, the F-test, Breusch-Pagan test, the Akaike information criterion and comparisons of in-sample predictions with observed values all confirm modelling choices.

Additional investments through funds are available in the IJGlobal (2019) database and are included in the unlisted fund estimations. Inclusion of the deal values in the deal estimations is straightforward as the information is available (as is the case Preqin data). As all funds involved in the deals are also in the Preqin database, the IJGlobal deals could be attributed through these funds.

Direct project-level investments

Data on direct project-level investments by institutional investors is sourced from IJGlobal (2019), Preqin (2020) and (OECD, 2018). This information on direct investment is merged to arrive at the overall direct investments by institutional investors, using manual merging and OpenRefine to avoid double-counting of investments. As in the case of unlisted funds, careful attention is paid to exclude past owners of assets.

The merged data provides information on 953 observed transactions with equity participation by an institutional investor. Due to missing values, equity investment are estimated for a portion of these transaction. To estimate the unobserved equity value, first a regression is run using information about the investors and the asset[28]. Next, gearing ratios[29] are applied to arrive at equity portions of deals, and percentage stakes acquired by investors are applied to arrive at the absolute value of direct institutional equity investment.

The merged data also provides information on 168 observed transactions involving debt provision by an institutional investor. Of these, 4% of the unobserved debt investment values are straightforwardly calculated based on observed information. For the remaining data gaps of 79% of the investments, values are estimated. An in-sample comparison reveals that the average of total observed debt investment share for a deal is a good approximation of the observed USD debt shares. Consequently 18% of the remaining missing values are replaced based on these averages. Missing data for the remaining 61% of observed deals are replaced by averages of investments in a peer-group based on asset, deal and investor characteristics, assuming representativeness of these groups. One final observed debt investment is dropped since no useful data for estimation was observed for this investment.

Listed funds and listed stocks

Investment data for publicly listed infrastructure funds and stocks is retrieved from Thomson-Reuters EIKON (Refinitiv, 2020).

For listed stocks of corporations, the EIKON data provides a list of investors and the percentage shares of investments in these companies. These shares are then multiplied by the market capitalisation as on last trading day of February 2020. All non-USD values are converted to USD equivalents using an average of the 2019 exchange rates from the EIKON database. These values combined with the investor information provide the investor-company-level information on investments, including the investment value. Further, EIKON provides a sector-classification, which is transferred into the classification presented in Annex 1.B.

For listed infrastructure funds the analysis starts by filtering all funds tagged as infrastructure in the Lipper funds database of EIKON. The available funds include listed mutual funds, INVITs and ETFs. Out of these 2000 funds, useful data exists for only 148 funds. The analysis is based on these 148 funds only since no useful information on the other funds is available to estimate their size as well as holdings or ownership composition. Fund holdings typically are equity shares (e.g. stocks), fixed income instruments (e.g. bonds) and cash. Rather than include all investments by these funds as infrastructure, the analysis includes only those fund holdings matching the infrastructure definition outlined in chapter 2 (see discussion in Box 2.1). Data on YieldCos and REITs has been treated similarly. Where possible, desk research is used to supplement EIKON data to increase comprehensiveness for the instruments. This is especially true for INVITs where most of the data is collected through desk research.

Note that overlap is avoided between institutional investors holdings through listed funds and direct institutional investor holdings in corporations. Since the direct holdings do not include holdings of listed fund shares, the funds' holdings are only included through the listed fund holdings. So while an institutional investor may hold shares of a corporation directly as well as through listed infrastructure funds, these are cumulative holdings rather than double-counted.

For all listed items, observed ownership and holdings are noticeably incomplete as they do not add up to 100% of shares. As is the nature of publicly traded data, information on details is largely available, but not always complete. This would indicate that the aggregates presented in chapter 2 are only a lower bound. However, typically data for large transactions and for large investors is systematically better tracked than for small investors or transactions. The analysis can reasonably assume that institutional investments in the stock market belong in these categories. Therefore the aggregates of chapter 2 for listed stocks should be a reasonable estimate of the actual value of institutional holdings of listed infrastructure stocks. For listed funds the same applies, with the exception of funds without data, for which the analysis has to stay agnostic.

Annex 2.B. Activities, Sub-Sector and Sector Classification

Table 2.B.1 below provides an overview of the activities, sub-sectors and sectors included in this report. The following table has been developed based on the classification found in Preqin (2020[3]), Thomson-Reuters (2020[2]) and IJGlobal (2019[4]). All infrastructure assets and corporate entities included in the dataset developed through the empirical mapping fall into one or more of the following activities.

Annex Table 2.B.1. Activities, sub-sectors and sectors of infrastructure

Activity	Sub-sector	Sector
Construction & Engineering	Construction	Construction (Multisector)
Electricity Generation Transmission and Distribution	T&D	Energy
Electric Utilities	Utilities	Energy
Gas storage, transportation and distribution	Fossil Fuels	Energy
Oil storage, transportation and distribution	Fossil Fuels	Energy
Gas Utilities	Fossil Fuels	Energy
Nuclear Power Company	Nuclear	Energy
Electric and Gas Utility	Utilities	Energy
Grid operator	T&D	Energy
Natural gas liquids company	Fossil Fuels	Energy
Renewable Utility	Renewables	Energy
Oil and Gas pipeline construction	Fossil Fuels	Energy
Natural gas processing	Fossil Fuels	Energy
Multiline Utility	Utilities	Energy
Electric Power and Heat	Utilities	Energy
Upstream infrastructure	Fossil Fuels	Energy
Midstream infrastructure	Fossil Fuels	Energy
Downstream infrastructure	Fossil Fuels	Energy
Renewable Energy Services	Renewables	Energy
Oil and Gas Refining and Marketing	Fossil Fuels	Energy
Fossil Fuel electric utilities	Fossil Fuels	Energy
Renewable IPPs	Renewables	Energy
Fossil Fuel IPPs	Fossil Fuels	Energy
Nuclear Utilities	Nuclear	Energy
Nuclear IPPs	Nuclear	Energy
Biomass/Biofuel facility	Bioenergy	Energy
Geothermal power	Geothermal	Energy
Hydro power	Hydro Power	Energy
Solar Power	Solar Power	Energy
Waste to energy	Bioenergy	Energy
Wind Power	Wind Power	Energy
Energy efficiency	Energy Efficiency	Energy
Natural resources infrastructure	Fossil Fuels	Energy
Coal-fired power plant	Fossil Fuels	Energy
Natural resources refineries	Fossil Fuels	Energy
Clean technology	Energy Efficiency	Energy
Natural resources pipelines	Fossil Fuels	Energy

Activity	Sub-sector	Sector
Natural resources storage facility	Fossil Fuels	Energy
Oil-fired plant	Fossil Fuels	Energy
Renewable and thermal infrastructure	Diversified	Energy
Renewable and conventional electricity	Diversified	Energy
Fire, Law and Order infrastructure	Law and Order Infrastructure	Social
Educational buildings	Education	Social
Government accommodation	Government Buildings	Social
Government buildings	Government Buildings	Social
Healthcare/Medical facilities	Healthcare	Social
Hospitals	Healthcare	Social
Judicial buildings	Government Buildings	Social
Parking lots	Other Social Infrastructure	Social
Police stations and training facilities	Law and Order Infrastructure	Social
Prisons	Law and Order Infrastructure	Social
Public buildings	Other Social Infrastructure	Social
Senior homes	Other Social Infrastructure	Social
Social housing	Other Social Infrastructure	Social
Student accommodation	Other Social Infrastructure	Social
Public library	Other Social Infrastructure	Social
Telecommunication infrastructure construction	Construction	Telecommunications
Satellite communications network	Satellite Infrastructure	Telecommunications
Wireless communication	Wireless Communication	Telecommunications
Optic fibre	Internet	Telecommunications
Mobile phone networks	Network	Telecommunications
Cellular towers	Wireless Communication	Telecommunications
Data centres	Internet	Telecommunications
Cable television networks	Network	Telecommunications
Landline phone networks	Network	Telecommunications
Marine cargo handling	Freight	Transport
Railroads	Railways	Transport
Roads	Roads	Transport
Sea Ports	Ports	Transport
Toll Roads	Roads	Transport
Tunnels	Roads	Transport
Highways	Roads	Transport
Maritime transport	Freight	Transport
Bridges	Roads	Transport
Heavy Rail	Freight	Transport
Multimodal Transport	Railways	Transport
Street Lighting	Street Lighting	Transport
Airports	Airports	Transport
Airport operator	Airports	Transport
Toll road management	Roads	Transport
Metro	Railways	Transport
Marine Logistics	Freight	Transport
Ground freight & logistics	Freight	Transport
Rail services	Railways	Transport
Railway freight	Freight	Transport
Freight trucking	Freight	Transport
Inland water freight	Freight	Transport
Deep sea freight	Freight	Transport
Air Freight	Freight	Transport

Activity	Sub-sector	Sector
Rolling stock	Railways	Transport
Highway and bridge construction	Construction	Transport
Waste management	Waste Management	Waste
Hazardous waste management	Waste Management	Waste
Sewage treatment plants	Sewage Treatment	Waste
Sewage utilities	Sewage Utilities	Waste
Waste disposal and recycling services	Waste Management	Waste
Irrigation systems	Water Distribution	Water
Water distribution	Water Distribution	Water
Water treatment	Water Treatment	Water
Water utilities	Water Utilities	Water
Desalination	Water Treatment	Water
Water and sewage infrastructure construction	Construction	Water

Source: Authors based on of (Preqin,2020), (Refinitiv, 2020) and (IJGlobal, 2019).

Annex 2.C. Identifying Green Infrastructure Sectors

The OECD defines infrastructure as "the system of public works in a country, state or region, including roads, utility lines and public buildings". This includes electricity generation, transmission and distribution assets. Table 2.C.1 below lists infrastructure-relevant sectors and technologies that qualify as 'green' under select sustainable finance taxonomies, green bond standards and/or guidelines (analysed resources) in select OECD and G20 jurisdictions. This exercise aims to highlight the lowest common denominator to develop a working definition of 'green infrastructure' for the sole purpose of the mapping in this report. To identify the lowest common denominator, all infrastructure-related sectors in the analysed resources are mapped alongside each other. The sectors that are accepted as green by all or most of the analysed resources are designated green for the purpose of this report. It must be noted that some analysed resources prescribe emissions or other thresholds for assets belonging to certain sectors while others don't. For instance passenger rail is unequivocally green according to the standards and definitions in Japan and China but maybe considered green as per the EU taxonomy only if the asset in question meets a stipulated threshold. Given the absence of granular emission-level data, it is difficult to overlay such a conditionality on the assets in this report's dataset. Therefore in the interest of facilitating analysis, wherever applicable, all assets in this report's dataset are assumed to meet the prescribed thresholds. In the Table below, sectors that are unequivocally green are indicated as dark green, sectors subject to a stipulated threshold are marked as light green. White or blank cells indicate absence of coverage.

With the exception of the Climate Bonds Initiative (CBI) taxonomy (which is a market-based taxonomy as distinct from an official, government-established taxonomy or definition), the taxonomies and standards/guidelines compared below do not explicitly exclude sectors. The taxonomies and standards/guidelines assessed only indicate sectors, and projects/activities therein, that qualify as 'green'. The extreme right column indicates the sectors in which institutional investment has been observed in the empirical mapping.

Annex Table 2.C.1. Infrastructure-relevant sectors and technologies that qualify as 'green' under select sustainable finance taxonomies

Sector	EU	CHN	IDN	ZAF	IND	JPN	BRA	ARG	CBI	Corresponding sectors with observed investments
Energy										**Energy**
Electricity Generation										
Solar PV										✓
Solar CSP										✓
Wind Power										✓
Marine Energy (Electricity)										
Hydropower *										✓
Geothermal Energy*										✓
Gas*										✓
Bioenergy*										✓
Electricity Transmission and Distribution System										
Grid*										✓
Direct Connection to LCEG										✓
Smart Grid**										
EV Charging Stations										
Electrification of Transport										
Energy Storage										
Electricity Storage*										
Thermal Energy Storage										
Hydrogen Storage*										
Other Transmission and Distribution Infrastructure										
Retrofit of Gas T&D*										
District Heating and Cooling*										
Water										**Water**
Collection, Treatment & Supply*										✓
Waste										**Waste**
Centr. Wastewater Treatment*										✓
Solid Waste Treatment										✓
Anaerobic Digestion										
Sewage Sludge*										
Bio-waste*										
Transport * **										**Transport**
Passenger Rail*										✓
Freight Rail*										✓
Metro, Light Rail, Tram, Bus										✓

Table Legend	Included	Included with qualifiers	Not included or addressed

Note: LCEG: Low-Carbon Electricity Generation ^ In addition to official, government-established standards/guidelines issued in select jurisdictions, the market-based taxonomy developed by Climate Bond Initiative (CBI) has also been considered due to its widespread use and adherence. * Eligibility is contingent upon fulfilling emission threshold and/or other criteria prescribed by the relevant standard/principle or taxonomy ** As per the China Green Bond Endorsed Project Catalogue (2015) Smart Grid refer "*to grid construction and operation or technical transformation and upgrading projects, which improve the balance and responsiveness of supply and demand, promote integrated energy efficiency of the grid, lower the transformation of power loss in transmission, and enhance the capability of renewables access*". *** Activities not included in the EU taxonomy so far: (i) Maritime shipping (including reference to EU MRV regime); (ii) Aviation; (iii) ICT for transport; (iv) Energy efficiency improvements in equipment and infrastructure (e.g. in ports); and (v) Research, development & innovation related activities having the potential to substantially decarbonize the transport sector. Guidelines by ARG (Argentina) prescribe the climate bond taxonomy as the reference for eligible green projects. For the purpose of the table above, the term renewable energy has been interpreted to refer to the technologies prescribed by the climate bond taxonomy.

Sources: http://www.greenfinance.org.cn/displaynews.php?cid=79&id=468;
https://www.djppr.kemenkeu.go.id/uploads/files/dmodata/in/6Publikasi/Offering%20Circular/ROI%20Green%20Bond%20and%20Green%20S
ukuk%20Framework.pdf;; https://www.sebi.gov.in/legal/circulars/may-2017/disclosure-requirements-for-issuance-and-listing-of-green-debt-
securities_34988.html; https://shaktifoundation.in/wp-content/uploads/2019/08/Building-a-Consensus-on-the-Definition-of-Green-Finance-
1.pdf; https://cmsportal.febraban.org.br/Arquivos/documentos/PDF/Guia_emissa%CC%83o_ti%CC%81tulos_verdes_ING.pdf;
http://www.env.go.jp/en/policy/economy/gb/en_greenbond_guideline2017.pdf;
https://www.boletinoficial.gob.ar/detalleAviso/primera/203933/20190322; https://www.climatebonds.net/taxonomy-green-definitions

Table 2.C.2 below compares the definition/meaning of the term 'green' under relevant standards/guidelines/principles prescribed by the competent authority* in select OECD and G20 jurisdictions. The objective is to highlight common elements to arrive at a working assumption for the meaning of 'green' for the purposes of this report.

Annex Table 2.C.2. Elements of 'Green' projects and activities

Jurisdiction	Consideration included under 'Green'	Instrument
China (CHN)	Projects that address climate change, environmental pollution, aggravated resource constraints and ecological degradation	China Green Bond Endorsed Project Catalogue (2015 Edition)
Indonesia (IDN)	Projects promoting transition to a low-emission economy and climate resilient growth including climate mitigation, adaptation and biodiversity	Green Bond and Green Sukuk Framework
India (IND)	Projects belonging to clean energy, clean transportation, sustainable water management, climate change adaptation, energy efficiency including green buildings, sustainable waste management, sustainable land use including sustainable forestry and agriculture, biodiversity and any other category prescribed by SEBI from time to time	SEBI (2017) Disclosure Requirements for Issuance and Listing of Green Debt Securities
Japan (JPN)	Projects with clear environmental benefits	Green Bond Guidelines, 2017
Argentina (ARG)	Projects or activities with environmental benefits including climate change mitigation, adaptation, biodiversity and/or natural resource conservation, pollution prevention (air, water and soil)	Guidelines for the issuance of social, green and sustainable securities in Argentina 2019
Brazil (BRA)	Projects or assets that have positive environmental or climate-related attributes	Guidelines for Issuing Green Bonds in Brazil 2016

Note: * The guidelines considered for Brazil are those issued jointly by the Brazilian Federation of Banks (FEBRABAN) and Brazilian Business Council for Sustainable Development (CEBDS).

Source:http://www.greenfinance.org.cn/displaynews.php?cid=79&id=468;
https://www.djppr.kemenkeu.go.id/uploads/files/dmodata/in/6Publikasi/Offering%20Circular/ROI%20Green%20Bond%20and%20Green%20S
ukuk%20Framework.pdf;; https://www.sebi.gov.in/legal/circulars/may-2017/disclosure-requirements-for-issuance-and-listing-of-green-debt-
securities_34988.html;
https://cmsportal.febraban.org.br/Arquivos/documentos/PDF/Guia_emissa%CC%83o_ti%CC%81tulos_verdes_ING.pdf;
http://www.env.go.jp/en/policy/economy/gb/en_greenbond_guideline2017.pdf;
https://www.boletinoficial.gob.ar/detalleAviso/primera/203933/20190322;

References

Amenc, N., F. Blanc-Brude and A. Chreng (2017), "The rise of "fake infra": The unregulated growth of listed infrastructure and the dangers it poses to the future of infrastructure investing". [11]

IJGlobal (2019), *IJ Global Infrastructure Transactions Database*. [4]

IJGlobal (2017), *IJGlobal - Transaction Data*, https://ijglobal.com/data/search-transactions (accessed on 4 December 2017). [13]

Infrastructure Investor (2020), *How digital infrastructure became 'mission-critical'*, https://www.infrastructureinvestor.com/how-digital-infrastructure-became-mission-critical/. [8]

OECD (2020), *OECD Glossary of Statistical Terms - Infrastructure Definition*. [5]

OECD (2018), *Financing water Investing in sustainable growth*. [9]

OECD (2018), *Innovation, Standardization and Data Collection for Long Term Investment: OECD Workshop on Data Collection for Long-term Investment – November 2018 -Summary record*, https://www.oecd.org/daf/fin/private-pensions/OECD-Workshop-on-Data-Collection-Summary-2018.pdf. [1]

OECD (2015), *Mapping Channels to Mobilise Institutional Investment in Sustainable Energy*, Green Finance and Investment, OECD Publishing, Paris, https://dx.doi.org/10.1787/9789264224582-en. [6]

Ofwat (2020), *Water sector overview*, https://www.ofwat.gov.uk/regulated-companies/ofwat-industry-overview/ (accessed on 21 September 2020). [10]

Preqin (2020), *Alternative Assets Data, Solutions and Insights*. [3]

Röttgers, D., A. Tandon and C. Kaminker (2018), "OECD Progress Update on Approaches to Mobilising Institutional Investment for Sustainable Infrastructure", *OECD Environment Working Papers*, No. 138, OECD Publishing, Paris, https://dx.doi.org/10.1787/45426991-en. [12]

Thomson-Reuters (2020), *EIKON*. [2]

UBS (2019), *Top infrastructure trends for 2020 | UBS Global topics*, https://www.ubs.com/global/en/asset-management/insights/asset-class-research/real-assets/2019/top-infrastructure-trends-for-2020.html (accessed on 17 June 2020). [7]

Notes

[1] As on end of February 2020

[2] Note that this report does not include Strategic Investment Funds (SIFs) due to lack of data. They would be a relevant addition as a vehicle for institutional investments, including those of Sovereign Wealth Funds (SWFs).

[3] Note that data on listed infrastructure investments was downloaded in late February 2020 and therefore before the COVID-19 crisis fully hit the stock markets. Data was not updated to post-COVID-19 for two reasons. First, an update of listed data would inevitably have happened during rather than after the crisis, i.e. it would be influenced by the crisis, but at the time of writing it would not have been possible to say to what extent. Second, as other data, e.g. unlisted funds data, is updated only periodically, an update of only the listed investment data would have been inconsistent.

[4] Investments at the time of an initial public offering could be an exception here, since capital raised may be used for new assets.

[5] While participation in primary issuances may provide investment for new asset creation, stock investments in the secondary market do not provide additional capital to the company concerned. Therefore an investment in an infrastructure company's stock does not cause a direct change in the real economy (except in the case of a primary issuance, i.e. a initial public offering). While these secondary market activities may provide incentives to engage in the primary activity of setting up corporations, this indirect effect is beyond the remit of this report.

[6] Where transaction data is more limited than on public exchanges

[7] Unlisted funds pool capital from multiple investors. Funds are typically structured as limited partnerships with an asset/fund manager (party raising capital) as the *general partner* and investors (including institutional investors) in the fund as *limited partners*. Funds have a fixed lifespan which may be extend by the consent of limited partners. During the investment period, limited partners are entitled to cash flow which may either be distributed or reinvested. Distributions are typically paid on a pro rata basis.

[8] Unless stated otherwise, the term YieldCo in this report refers generally to the legal structure that enables securitising illiquid physical assets, and not to any particular vehicle or strategy in existence in the market either presently or at any time in the past.

[9] Infrastructure Investment Trusts (INVITs) and master limited partnerships (MLPs), like YieldCos, combine access to infrastructure cash-flow with liquidity. INVITs and infrastructure REITs are publicly traded trusts that own and operate infrastructure assets. MLPs are particular to the United States. They are pass through vehicles for tax purposes and are for the use in infrastructure restricted by law to activities related to natural resource exploitation.

[10] 'Non-green assets' excludes the following infrastructure sectors for which climate and other environmental implications are not quite as clear: telecommunications infrastructure, roads, bridges, tunnels, highways.

[11] Vintages of some funds in the underlying data are uncertain and have been excluded from the calculation for the sake of precision. However, when the amount held through funds with uncertain vintages is factored in, the estimate of capital locked in non-green assets rises by USD 100 billion.

[12] 'Non-green assets' excludes the following infrastructure sectors for which climate and other environmental implications are not quite as clear: telecommunications infrastructure, roads, bridges, tunnels, highways.

[13] Vintages of some funds in the underlying data are uncertain and have been excluded from the calculation for the sake of precision. However, when the amount held through funds with uncertain vintages are factored in, the estimate of capital locked in non-green assets rises by USD 20.5 billion.

[14] 'Non-green assets' excludes the following infrastructure sectors for which climate and other environmental implications are not quite as clear: telecommunications infrastructure, roads, bridges, tunnels, highways.

[15] Exchange Traded Funds (ETFs) are a mix between open-ended and closed-end funds. Like closed-end funds, units of ETFs trade on public exchanges. However, like open-ended funds, ETFs are always open for new subscription i.e. new units are created and the fund size expands based on new demand. Redemption by investors leads to contraction of the fund size.

[16] Note here that energy efficiency included here does not include energy efficient real estate.

[17] An availability payment is a contractual payment, as part of an offtake agreement, usually by the public sector in PPP formats.

[18] Economic dispersion in revenues due to variations in end-user demand.

[19] The difference between the aggregate of the far left and far right side of Figure 2.11 are due to rounding.

[20] Note that since these services are water-related, some of these investments may be captured in the water utilities category of Figure 2.11.

[21] Note here that due to the choice of country scope of this report, some other SWFs from the Middle East are not reflected.

[22] While the data gathered for this report represents the current stock (holdings) of investment and not flows (i.e. time series data), evolving risk appetite of investors can be ascertained from the vintages of unlisted funds. Capital commitments by asset owners, vintages and strategies of funds together suggest a trend.

[23] Note that to avoid overlap, each single deal added from the IJGlobal database is manually checked against deals from the Preqin database.

[24] Note that missing data on called percentage values for observed funds was replaced by the average called percentage. While not exact, this approach is reasonable given the narrow distribution of called percentage values around the average.

[25] Note that missing data on RVPI is replaced by averaging over observed RVPI values of gradually widening peer-groups of funds. Factors used to identify peer-groups include the size of the investor in terms of AUM, the year of the fund as well as the country, strategy and core industry target of the fund in question.

[26] Other information included in the regression underlying the prediction are country of origin of the investor, the investor type (asset managers, private pension funds, public pension funds, insurance companies, sovereign wealth funds, investment companies and funds of funds), other funds invested in by the investor, as well as fixed effects of the investor and fund.

[27] Note that investments recorded in Preqin (2020) in currencies other than USD were converted to USD using OECD National Accounts (2020) data.

[28] Information included in the regression underlying the prediction are country of origin of the investor, the investor type as well as the country, year and industry of the investment.

[29] Note that data gaps for gearing ratios and acquired stakes are filled using averaging of the observed values by peer-groups. Similar to the averaging procedure for missing values estimated for private equity data, the peer-group categories are gradually relaxed if there is no relevant peer-group over which to average.

3 Pathways and levers to scale-up institutional investment in green infrastructure

The previous chapter 2 shows the relevance of unlisted funds and direct investments for asset owners and the importance of the securitised instruments YieldCos, infrastructure REITs and INVITs for asset managers to shift and scale up institutional investment in infrastructure. Based on that mapping of current holdings, this chapter develops a framework to identify levers and policy priorities to shift and accelerate institutional investment in green infrastructure. Important levers exist for both investors and policymakers. Interventions to scale up investment through unlisted funds and direct investment should aim to target investment-decision making by asset owners. Interventions to scale-up investment through securitised instruments should aim to target investment-decision making by asset managers. Policymakers can employ a set of measures to accelerate institutional investment in green infrastructure. These include establishing an enabling policy environment, clarifying fiduciary duty, supporting institutional innovation, to active de-risking and public-private initiatives, and facilitating securitisation of infrastructure assets.

In the context of shifting and accelerating institutional investment in infrastructure assets that are aligned with global climate and development objectives, the empirical mapping provides three key takeaways:

1. The lion's share of current investment holdings is held through unlisted funds, direct project-level equity/debt and securitised vehicles;
2. Asset owners demonstrate a preference towards illiquid infrastructure instruments;
3. Asset managers exhibit a preference towards liquid infrastructure instruments.

Using these findings as a point of departure, this chapter shifts to the perspective of policy-makers to provide guidance on how to mobilise larger amounts of institutional capital towards green assets. It begins with a brief discussion of the barriers to institutional investment in green infrastructure as identified in existing literature. The chapter then goes on to form an analytical framework, building on relevant barriers and empirical evidence from chapter 2. The framework identifies levers and policy priorities to upscale investment in green infrastructure. This is followed by a consideration of the role of policy-making in upscaling institutional investment in green infrastructure.

Barriers to institutional investment in infrastructure

A rich body of literature points to a variety of factors that impede institutional investment (OECD, 2015[1]; Kaminker et al., 2013[2]; Nelson and Pierpont, 2013[3]; Kaminker, Stewart and Upton, 2012[4]; Blended Finance Taskforce, 2018[5]). From currency and transfer risks to political risk, an investor will face different permutations of challenges depending on the jurisdiction of investment. Regulations in an investor's home jurisdiction, for instance quantitative limits on cross border holdings, may further compound the challenge. Figure 3.1 presents a composite (although not comprehensive) view of the barriers to institutional investment. Notably, many barriers in Figure 3.1 have an effect on price incentives, such as a lack of or low carbon prices. While barriers are not the focus of this report, certain barriers are discussed where relevant in this chapter. Figure 3.1's sources give an overview over all barriers mentioned as well.

Figure 3.1.Barriers to institutional investment in green infrastructure

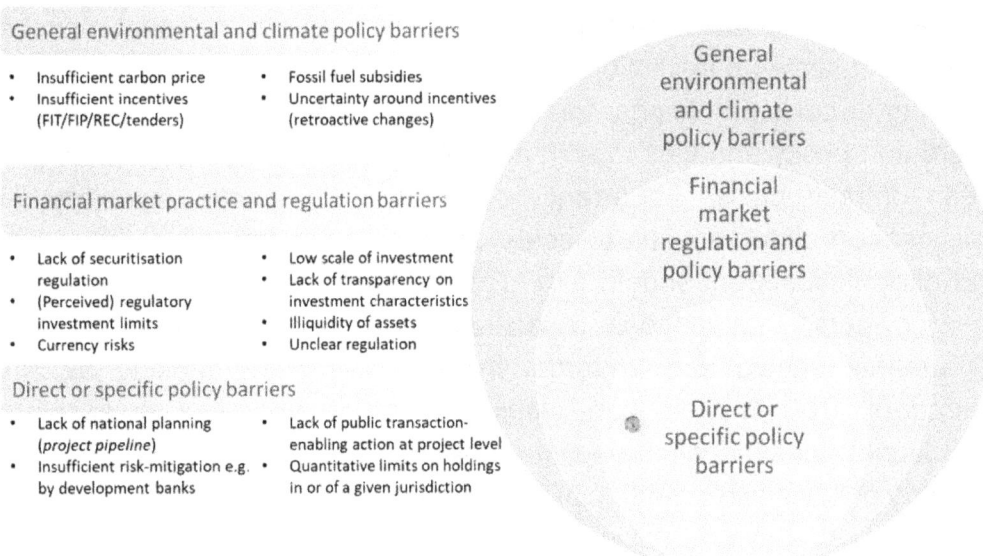

General environmental and climate policy barriers
- Insufficient carbon price
- Insufficient incentives (FIT/FIP/REC/tenders)
- Fossil fuel subsidies
- Uncertainty around incentives (retroactive changes)

Financial market practice and regulation barriers
- Lack of securitisation regulation
- (Perceived) regulatory investment limits
- Currency risks
- Low scale of investment
- Lack of transparency on investment characteristics
- Illiquidity of assets
- Unclear regulation

Direct or specific policy barriers
- Lack of national planning (project pipeline)
- Insufficient risk-mitigation e.g. by development banks
- Lack of public transaction-enabling action at project level
- Quantitative limits on holdings in or of a given jurisdiction

General environmental and climate policy barriers

Financial market regulation and policy barriers

Direct or specific policy barriers

Source: Authors based on (OECD, 2015[1]; Ang, Röttgers and Burli, 2017[6]; OECD, 2017[7]; OECD, 2018[8]; G20/OECD, 2013[9])

Developing an analytical framework to greening institutional investment

The 3 key takeaways (from the empirical mapping) cited at the beginning of this chapter highlight a relationship between asset owners/asset managers and the instruments they prefer to use for green infrastructure investment. The majority of green infrastructure investment by asset owners is held through unlisted funds and in project-level equity/debt. The main means for scaling up green infrastructure investment by asset owners is to influence their investment decision-making by encouraging investment in the channels for which they have most appetite and room to expand investment: unlisted funds and direct investment. This relationship is the primary conduit (see Figure 3.2.) for scaling up investment in these channels. At the same time, asset managers can be encouraged to expand investment in these channels, despite their main focus on liquidity. Asset managers' investment decision-making with respect to unlisted funds and direct investment is a secondary conduit for scaling up investment in these channels (see Figure 3.2). Similarly, to upscale investment through securitised structures, policy and other interventions should target investment activities by asset managers (primary conduit). The distinctions in Figure 3.2 provide the basis of the analytical framework for this chapter, as they help identify potential pathways to scale investment. They are simplified, drawn for ease of analysis, and are not intended to be interpreted beyond the context of this report. Though other instruments and mechanisms exist, the focus of this chapter is levers and policy action to increase green infrastructure deployment by scaling investments through unlisted funds, direct investment and securitised structures (most relevant in this chapter: YieldCos, infrastructure REITs and INVITs).

Figure 3.2. Schematic view of currently-preferred investment instruments and means for influencing institutional infrastructure investment

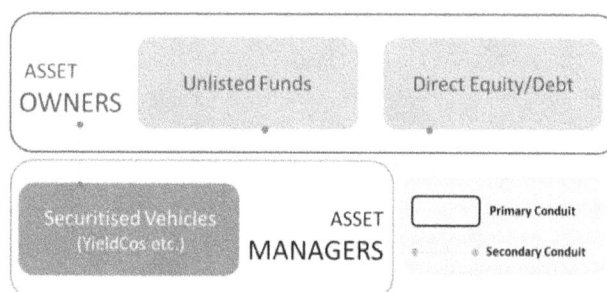

Note: This figure has been developed for the sole purpose to facilitate analysis and should not be interpreted beyond the context of this report. The analysis presented below focuses on primary influence only.
Source: Authors

Based on Figure 3.2, Figure 3.3 proposes a framework to pinpoint levers for policy-makers and investors, as well as related pathways from policy action to investments.[1] For the three instruments unlisted funds, direct equity/debt and securitised vehicles, the framework below presents a deconstructed view of the elements of the investment process mapped in Chapter 2. The framework highlights key elements at each step of the investment process and connects them with relevant policy areas and actors (not limited to asset owners and asset managers). In particular, the framework is intended to focus attention on key action areas to accelerate the flow of institutional capital towards green infrastructure assets. Figure 3.3 should be read as a description of the ecosystem of institutional investment in green infrastructure and not as a flow chart with sequential actions or relationships. The framework aims to demonstrate how the various components of the investment ecosystem relate to, interact with and influence each other.

Figure 3.3. Framework to identify key levers to "green" institutional investment in infrastructure

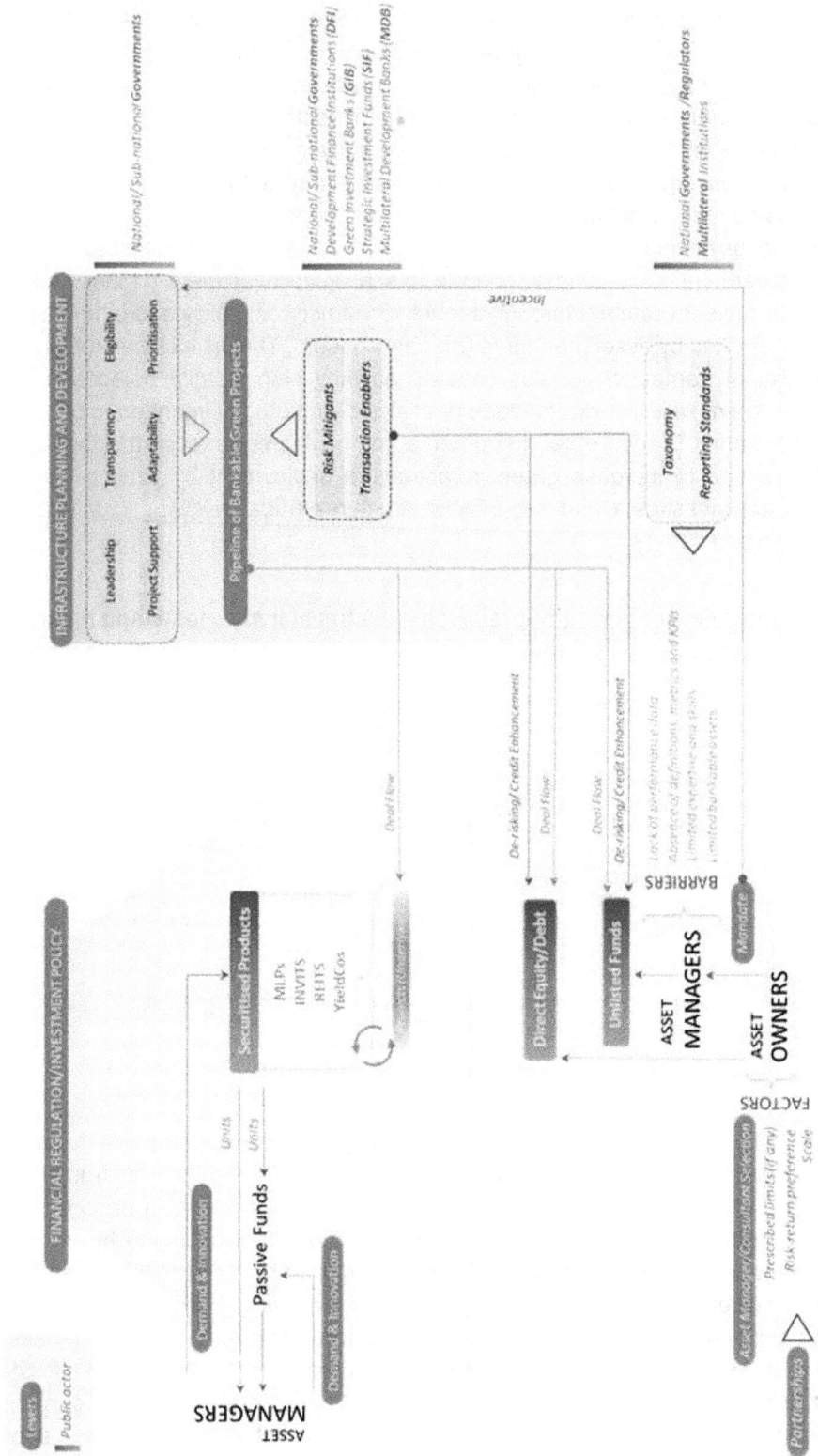

Note: Asset Owners may invest in units of securitised vehicles and passive funds directly. The framework above has been simplified to aid analysis.
Source: Authors

The framework in Figure 3.3 highlights **three pathways** to scale green infrastructure investments which are interlinked and can be combined: **Green project pipelines**, **Mandates**, and **Securitised products**.

Green pipelines: Policymakers create an environment that enables origination of investment-grade ("bankable") green projects and allows development of a project pipeline. This ensures deal flow for asset owners (looking to invest directly in projects) and private infrastructure funds.

The **levers** related to **green pipelines** are:

- **Infrastructure planning and development policies;**
- **Enabling investor partnerships.**

Mandates: Policymakers clarify fiduciary duty in relation to green investments. This would allow and encourage asset owners to issue greener mandates to asset managers.

The **lever** for this pathway is

- **Financial regulation and investment policies (in particular clarifying fiduciary duty)**

Securitised products: Policymakers allow securitised products like INVITs and YieldCos.[2] Project sponsors and short-term financiers off-load operating projects through securitisation, allowing early-stage investors to reinvest in new projects. Units of securitised vehicles may be privately placed[3] with institutional investors or publicly offered. Public offering of units (at stock exchanges), allows participation by a wider set of investors beyond asset managers, e.g. retail investors and defined contribution pension plans. Bringing in these two groups of investors more systematically could enlarge the pool of capital available for infrastructure development. In addition to providing a demand side push by investing on behalf of their clients, asset managers may include units of securitised infrastructure vehicles in passive funds and index products to increase sustainable finance offerings.

The **levers** associated with **securitised products** are:

- **Demand and innovation – Enabling frameworks for securitisation**;
- **Demand and innovation – Institutional investors as 'recyclers of capital'**; and
- **Demand and innovation – Leveraging the trend towards passive investment**.

The following sections discuss in greater detail how these two pathways and related levers can scale-up investments, including the cross-cutting issue of public policies and direct public action. These sections focus on applications within relevant classes of investment instruments.

Green pipelines: Infrastructure planning and infrastructure development policies

Policy action is central to planning and developing infrastructure projects. This planning and coordination activity, incentivised and carried out by public agencies and ministries, provides information, orientation and a long-term investment view for investors. (OECD, 2018[8]) provides a detailed analysis of six factors to establish and strengthen green project pipelines: leadership; transparency; eligibility criteria; project support; prioritisation; and dynamic adaptability (see Table 3.1). Bespoke de-risking by public financial institutions and institutional innovation (e.g. Green Investment Banks (OECD, 2016[10]; OECD, 2018[8])) can be jointly viewed as the seventh factor to establish a pipeline of investment-grade assets and attract institutional capital towards critical infrastructure projects.

Table 3.1. Overview of factors to develop robust project pipelines

Factor	Factor Description
Leadership	Governments and other agencies championing the development of a robust project pipeline
Transparency	Transparent decision-making processes that inform investment
Prioritisation	Expediting, optimising strategically-valuable projects and shepherding them through development processes
Project Support	Provision of public funds and institutional support to overcome investment barriers
Eligibility Criteria	Setting criteria and conditions to systematically identify, assess and promote eligible projects
Dynamic Adaptability	Flexibility to adjust infrastructure to changing conditions so that investments remain pertinent over time

Source: Adapted from (OECD, 2018[8])

Asset owners and direct investment

Through direct equity and debt positions, pension funds, insurance companies and sovereign wealth funds (SWFs) hold an aggregated USD 62 billion in green infrastructure. The decision to invest directly at the project-level is a function of a variety of factors that are individual to an investor, for instance, risk-return objectives, skill and internal capacity. Regardless, from a systemic standpoint the unavailability of sufficient investment grade projects is a cross-cutting limitation. This limitation affects all types of existing and potential investors looking for projects or products where projects are bundled. As has been noted in the literature, it is the absence of enough investment-grade projects with attractive risk-adjusted returns, and not a lack of capital, that is a major impediment to green infrastructure investment (for an overview see OECD (2018[8])).

Infrastructure assets are operationally intensive and require methods of analysis distinct from traditional assets such as bonds and corporate stocks. For instance, fair values are appraised rather than observed. Infrastructure assets also often need specialist knowledge of local conditions for their effective management. Investing in illiquid infrastructure can therefore warrant developing specific skills and capacity, including in some cases establishing local presence, both by asset owners (in case of internal investment management) and asset managers. The costs of capacity and skill development are difficult to justify for a one-off opportunity. A pipeline of investment-grade projects and a government's clear commitment to environmental policy goals signal continued green investment opportunities. More importantly, they attract multiple interested investors, indicate exit possibilities and facilitate an active market for infrastructure assets.

Asset owners and unlisted funds

Like for direct investments by asset owners, a large limitation to infrastructure investing (green and otherwise) through unlisted funds, is insufficient deal flow (pipeline of investment-grade projects). The amount of committed, but unallocated capital in unlisted infrastructure funds (dry powder) grew at a rate of 15.5%[4] year-on-year from 2015 to 2019. At the end of Q2 2020, the committed, but unallocated capital equalled 38%[5] of total capital raised. For infrastructure funds, this is synonymous with a lack of investment-grade projects which would otherwise be an investment opportunity. Low returns on traditional assets like bonds or corporate stocks, persistently low interest rates and increased capital raising for new funds have led to high valuations for unlisted infrastructure (UBS, 2019[11]).

In-depth interviews for this report confirm that heightened competition for attractive risk-adjusted returns has made it increasingly difficult to access green infrastructure assets, as more investors look to accommodate infrastructure within their portfolios. Viewed through a demand-supply lens, having limited supply of investment-grade projects contributes to high valuations and depresses overall returns-this discourages investment.

From a policy standpoint a pipeline of investment-grade projects can ease some of these effects and spur investment. There is a rising interest in infrastructure investment. Despite the economic headwinds from COVID-19, infrastructure fundraising overall continues to be on a steady trajectory, though the picture may be more nuanced for subsets of specialised funds. Q1 2020 recorded the third highest amount of quarterly capital raised (albeit with notable regional differences) (Prequin, 2020[12]). An enabling policy environment facilitating a robust pipeline of green assets in each country seeking investment, coupled with the increasing focus by asset owners on green investments, could be a powerful combination to capitalise this momentum and accelerate green infrastructure investment. However, the challenge of strengthening enabling environments and establishing an investment-grade policy framework in each country where investment is needed is far from being met.[6]

Green pipelines: Enabling investor partnerships

Policy-makers in infrastructure-related agencies and public financial institutions can play a key role in accelerating investment by actively promoting and partaking in investor partnerships. Aside from co-investing, policy-makers could take on other enabling roles. For instance, they can create strategic investment funds (SIFs) and collaborate closely with the financial sector to address specific barriers to investing.

Asset owners, direct investment and unlisted funds

Asset owners with their long investment horizons are in a unique position to foster new and emerging sectors, such as off-shore wind. Partnerships between asset owners, in particular pension funds and life insurance companies, are proving to be an effective way to share risks, lower cost of capital, develop specialised capabilities and unlock long-term patient capital (Bachher, Jagdeep Singh, Adam Dixon, 2016[13]).

The example of the Danish wind industry is instructive for risk-sharing through partnerships, in the case of on-shore and also recently off-shore. Collaboration between Danish pension funds, supported by incentives from the government, was instrumental in developing collective know-how, expertise and mainstreaming the sector. A notable example is the 2011 deal for the 400 MW Anholt offshore wind farm, in which PensionDanmark and PKA together acquired 50% at EUR 900 million (Clean Energy Pipeline, 2014[14]). The Pension Infrastructure Platform in the United Kingdom is another example of the efficacy of partnerships in steering capital towards critical infrastructure aligned with environmental goals. Other initiatives focused on accelerating institutional investment in green infrastructure may encourage other types of partnerships and other means of up-scaling institutional investment.[7]

Investor partnerships can be instrumental in achieving scale, lowering transaction costs and fostering new sectors. Partnerships between governments and investors could accelerate origination of investment-grade projects and in turn, private investment. An emerging example of this approach is the concept of partnerships between general insurers, governments and life insurers. Broadly speaking, private infrastructure is typically insured by general insurers who, owing to their short-term liabilities, do not invest in infrastructure assets. Investments in infrastructure are largely provided by life insurance companies. While general insurers underwrite private infrastructure, public infrastructure assets are largely uninsured (they are self-insured by the government). This elevates the risk profile of public assets. In-depth interviews with experts point to ongoing efforts to establish partnerships between the insurance and public sectors to allow the two to work together across the entire lifecycle of projects. Working closely with governments, general insurers can develop bespoke products to underwrite public assets thereby lowering perceived risks for these assets and attracting investment from life insurance companies and other investors.

Mandates: Greening mandates

One key policy angle for greening infrastructure investments by institutional investors is to encourage greener mandates provided by asset owners, or a greener choice of investment consultants used by asset owners (as discussed below). While policy-makers do not have a direct influence on mandates, a clarification of fiduciary duty in relation to green infrastructure can encourage investment. The role of regulators and other policy-makers here would be to provide clarification on the relationship between fiduciary duty, duty of care and consideration of climate-related and other environment-related risks (UNEP FI, PRI, 2019[15]; Climate-Related Market Risk Subcommittee, 2020[16]). In-depth stakeholder interviews carried out for this report confirm this view. Adjustments or clarifications regarding fiduciary duty would create space for willing investors to make green infrastructure investments -- investors who otherwise may be reticent due to the risk of a breach in fiduciary duty.

Asset owners and unlisted funds

Asset owners and asset managers share a principal-agent relationship. Asset owners acting as limited partners play a critical role in the strategic asset allocation decisions of unlisted funds through the mandates they issue (PRI, 2018[17]). Asset owners have a determining influence on the priorities of asset managers and the overall industry. This is evidenced by the recent proliferation of sustainable investment funds—in 2019, 360 new sustainable investment funds were launched in Europe alone (Morningstar, 2020[18]). In addition, 250 European funds were repurposed from traditional to sustainable (Morningstar, 2020[18]).

Asset owners have a powerful tool in their mandates to support green infrastructure investment. According to 85 % of the respondents to a recent survey of hedge fund managers, demand from institutional investors is the foremost driver of ESG and therefore also green infrastructure investing (KPMG, AIMA, 2020[19]). At the same time, investment data tracked for this report shows consistently higher capital allocations by unlisted funds to non-green assets. Given that unlisted infrastructure funds invest in line with the mandate from limited partners (i.e. asset owners or asset managers investing in the funds), this points to the need for greening mandates. Interviews conducted for this report support this view.

A critical juncture to integrate climate and development objectives in investment decisions is the selection of asset managers and investment consultants. An increasing number of asset owners retain consultants for a range of functions from portfolio construction to asset manager selection. The growing role of investment consultants in capital allocation makes them important actors to accelerate green infrastructure investments. Despite rising recognition of the materiality of environmental and other non-financial risks to investments, there appears to be a continued disconnect with the services asset owners demand of their consultants and managers (PRI, 2017[20]).

Securitised products: Demand and innovation – Enabling frameworks for securitisation

Creating an enabling regulatory framework for securitised products targeted at green infrastructure would aid deal flow and help capitalise the rising interest in infrastructure in favour of green asset. Though the role of policymakers in structuring securitised vehicles is limited, regulations permitting securitised products and active de-risking (as in the case of UK Greencoat YieldCo) can encourage mainstreaming. The recent adoption of INVITs in India are a prime example of the efficacy of securitised products in monetising assets and freeing capital for new asset creation.

Asset managers and securitised structures: Extending the investor base to DC plans and retail investors

Apart from asset owners, asset managers also invest on behalf of a variety of other investors with a preference for liquidity, low risk, e.g. retail investors and individual savers who are members of defined contribution schemes. Globally there is an increasing shift from defined benefit (DB) to defined contribution (DC) pension schemes (Broadbent and Palumbo, 2006[21]). By the end of June 2019, total assets in DC plans in the United States alone amounted to USD 8.2 trillion (28% of all pension assets in the United States) (NAPA, 2019[22]). Defined contribution[8] plans represent a vast pool of long-term patient capital. However, as investment decisions are taken by the intended beneficiary[9] instead of a trustee, possible sizes of investment are much smaller. Unlike DB plans, DC plans do not allow for allocating large sums of capital -- from hundreds or thousands of investors -- to a single investment.

Securitised vehicles like YieldCos, REITs and INVITs offer a possible channel to scale-up infrastructure investment through defined contribution plans. As per the empirical mapping presented in chapter 2, asset managers currently hold USD 128.6 billion of renewables through YieldCos – over 70% of their total investment in green infrastructure. The available investment data does not shed light on the share of YieldCo investments on behalf of DC assets. However, the investment characteristics of YieldCos align well with retirement-focused long-term investing. In addition, YieldCos, REITs and INVITs provide liquid access to physical assets with regular distributions and opportunities for capital appreciation. This liquidity is necessary, as DC beneficiaries can alter their allocations periodically. Further, securitised structures offer exposure to operationally intensive assets without the need for any specialised skill, monitoring and oversight by the unit-holders. Securitised vehicles can offer a good fit to DC beneficiaries, thereby expanding the set of investors that can invest in infrastructure.

Traditional assets have posted declining returns since the aftermath of the 2008 global financial crisis. The COVID-19 pandemic is expected to compound this trend, highlighting the need for including alternatives with higher returns in long-term portfolios. Current market conditions provide fertile ground for the uptake of financially viable distribution-based vehicles[10], especially given their low correlation to traditional assets. (Wilshire Funds Management, 2016[23]) provide empirical evidence that inclusion of REITs and other high-yielding assets in DC plans can increase returns without elevating total risk. To support green infrastructure investment, policymakers could evaluate allowing inclusion of liquid alternatives in DC plan offerings. Asset managers could welcome the opportunity to provide innovative and green investment options.

Securitised products: Demand and innovation – Institutional investors as 'recyclers of capital'

The case for securitised vehicles is also linked to the role of institutional investors as 'recyclers of capital'. With their long investment horizons, institutional investors are well suited to free scarce construction stage risky capital for new investments. Project sponsors and other short-term investors can monetise operating assets by offloading them to the balance sheets of institutional investors. Mainstreaming YieldCos, INVITs and similar structures as instruments for this offloading process can be a helpful tool for bundling, scaling up and selling infrastructure investment. As highlighted in Figure 3.3, financial regulation including on securitised products is a key lever to shift and scale-up capital flows towards critical green infrastructure.

It is important to recall, however, that the financial viability and attractiveness of securitised structures are, at their core, a function of the soundness of the underlying assets. Steady supply of quality projects is critical to scaling-up securitised vehicles. In this respect, investment and infrastructure planning as well as infrastructure development policies are essential levers to shift and scale-up capital flows towards critical green infrastructure. They make a steady supply of projects much more feasible.

Securitised products: Demand and innovation – Leveraging the trend towards passive investment

There is a changing paradigm within the asset management industry, from active to passive strategies (Bloomberg, 2019[24]). Securitised vehicles with green infrastructure projects as the underlying assets can both leverage and contribute to this trend. Including more YieldCos, and other distribution-based vehicles like INVITs, in infrastructure indices and passive infrastructure ETFs can provide the means for a strong demand side push from asset managers. Inclusion of such vehicles would facilitate mainstreaming. Additionally, the availability of such liquid vehicles holding green infrastructure assets can aid creation of more passive ESG/sustainable investment products, possibly bringing in additional investors.

Providing a common understanding of 'green'

A corollary to the rising focus on infrastructure and green investments is increasing attention to the definition of 'green'. The present landscape of sustainable finance definitions and standards is a diverse one marked by the coexistence of a variety of standards, definitions and guidelines both from the public and private sector (Martini and Youngman, 2020[25]).

More precise and consistent definitions of which investments are "green" could facilitate investment by giving confidence and assurance to investors, and avoid market fragmentation. Additional benefits could include easier tracking of green infrastructure investment to measure them or tailor policy actions to these investments. The current debate around the increased certainty on the environmental sustainability of different types of investments and economic activities makes clear that a common understanding of what is green infrastructure is key (Martini and Youngman, 2020[25]). Policy makers may have an interest in coordinating on issues around taxonomies and definitions, and could apply multiple tools, ranging from binding taxonomy to voluntary guidelines. A common understanding, developed in collaboration with industry stakeholders, would facilitate more straightforward communication and decision-making regarding investments and accelerating investment flows.

Further regulatory measures to increase transparency regarding "non-green" investments could highlight risks related to investments in fossil fuel-based or environmentally detrimental investments. Regulatory measures increasing transparency of these risks for investors could include the implementation of recommendations of the Task-Force on Climate-Related Financial Disclosures (Task Force on Climate-related Financial Disclosure, 2017[26]), ESG-related regulation, a *brown* taxonomy (see also Martini and Youngman (2020[25])) or forward-looking climate scenario analysis.

Direct public action through financial and institutional innovation

Direct action by public financial institutions is already used effectively to mobilise private and commercial capital towards policy objectives. Tapping into the full potential of this ability is more important in times of budgetary and fiscal constraints. In addition to financial regulation and investment and infrastructure development policies, the public sector can unlock private investment through financial and institutional innovation.

A range of tools and techniques are available to governments and other public actors to mitigate project-level risks (see box 3.2). From anchor investments and grants to blending and guarantees, public actors can use a suite of instruments to credit enhance projects and attract institutional investors (Röttgers, Tandon and Kaminker, 2018[27]). The choice of de-risking instruments is broadly guided by the extent of liability assumed by public funds. From first loss tranches over loans and guarantees to grants, the risk assumption by public funds can span a broad spectrum. Shrinking fiscal space and debt ceilings in many countries have however, reduced the latitude of public interventions (Wai, Cheng and Pitterle, 2018[28]; Roy, Heuty and Letouzé, 2007[29]; International Monetary Fund, 2018[30]). Governments can be reluctant to provide guarantees for infrastructure projects or may not be able to provide the concessional capital or other public support needed to promote nascent sectors. In this environment, it is critical for public funds to be used in a manner that: maximises the amount of private money leveraged; effectively demonstrates the attractiveness and feasibility of investments; and builds self-sustaining markets poised to expand significantly after de-risking and other supporting measures are phased out.

Institutional innovation provides one more avenue. Institutional innovation can include setting-up a (public) green investment bank (GIB), a green window in an existing DFI, or a strategic investment fund (SIF). GIBs are specialised entities with a targeted and dynamic mandate (OECD, 2017[31]). This allows them to design and deploy a variety of interventions to respond to evolving market needs. While the mandate of GIBs can vary depending on the country context, it is the flexibility and latitude for innovation that makes them agile and effective in fostering new sectors and leveraging private investment (OECD, 2016[32]) (see box 3.1). An alternative to establishing a GIB is creating a 'green window' within an existing development finance institution, for instance as seen in India (Ministry of New and Renewable Energy, Government of India, 2019[33]). Through this approach, the existing sectoral, operational and institutional expertise of DFIs is leveraged to deploy bespoke green interventions in priority sectors.

Another approach is establishing SIFs. A SIF is a fund created to invest alongside private investors in priority sectors. Modelled along the lines of private equity funds, SIFs operate to mobilise private capital towards policy objectives while maintaining a commercial focus (Halland et al., 2016[34]). In many countries SIFs (e.g. Ireland Strategic Investment Fund) actively originate deals and focus on greenfield infrastructure. By carefully considering the purpose and mandate of an SIF, policymakers can effectively crowd-in private money (OECD, 2020[35]), lower investment risk and eventually cost of capital.

In addition to governments, multilateral financial institutions play an important role in mitigating risks and catalysing investment (Röttgers, Tandon and Kaminker, 2018[27]). MDBs may develop initiatives and facilities by themselves or jointly with the private sector- a relatively new approach. Public-private initiatives, such as those developed in the CPI Global Innovation Lab[11] or the World Bank Group's Scaling Solar programme[12] are examples of this, as is the recently launched "FAST-Infra" (Finance to Accelerate the Sustainable Transition – Infrastructure) initiative[13].

Box 3.1.Accelerating investment in green infrastructure- role of GIBs in creating secondary markets

Accelerating green infrastructure investment requires interventions on both the supply and the demand side. While much attention is paid to the need of improving supply of assets (creating pipelines of investment-grade projects), demand side interventions must evolve in tandem to foster an infrastructure investment ecosystem that efficiently allocates capital at the pace and scale needed. The central idea here is matching the right kind of investor with the appropriate project risk.

Every stage of a project's lifecycle carries different types of risks. For instance, during the construction stage a project has an elevated risk profile that is unsuitable for institutional and retail investors. Short-term financiers like project developers and banks have a higher risk tolerance (i.e. are willing to take on higher levels of risk in exchange for higher returns) and are much better placed to fund construction. However, once a project is operational, its risk profile becomes more acceptable to long-term investors like pension funds and insurance companies. At that stage, the project can be re-financed by these investors, freeing up scarce project development finance for other projects. Secondary markets play a key role to activate this concept of 'recycling capital'. As discussed below, a well-functioning secondary market for infrastructure is pivotal to offload operational assets to long-term investors and recycle capital. Efficient secondary markets could optimise risk pricing and reduce the overall cost of capital for infrastructure projects.

The public sector has a role to play in developing secondary markets for sustainable infrastructure. Australia's Clean Energy Finance Corporation (CEFC) and New York State's Green Bank provide two such examples.

Creating Secondary Markets for Sustainable Infrastructure in Australia – The Role of CEFC

In 2018, the National Australia Bank (NAB) bundled eight loans it had extended to seven renewable energy projects, into a portfolio worth AUD 200 million. The bank packaged 75% of the portfolio into a close-ended investment vehicle that issued project bonds to private investors, including institutional investors. CEFC made an AUD 90 million cornerstone investment in the offering to catalyse institutional investors. Insurance Australia Group, the largest insurance company in Australia, invested AUD 50 million alongside CEFC. In a first for Australia, the NAB low-carbon shared portfolio provided institutional investors an opportunity to get exposure to clean energy infrastructure without investing in single projects directly. The loan repayments provided by underlying projects are passed-through to institutional investors and other bondholders. NAB retained 25% of the portfolio on its own balance sheet and absorbed the management costs. The transaction allowed NAB to free-up capital to finance new projects by shifting assets to investors with commensurate risk appetite.

Creating Secondary Markets for Sustainable Infrastructure in US – The Role of NY Green Bank

Launched in 2014, the NY Green Bank has a specialised mandate to leverage private capital and expand clean energy markets. To that end, the NY Green Bank provides long-term refinancing to clean energy projects with merchant risk to facilitate their acquisition. The NY Green Bank targets operational projects that do not benefit from long-term offtake agreements and are exposed to market risk. More specifically, NY Green Bank refinances projects along with commercial banks in order to demonstrate the viability of long-term refinancing of clean energy projects with merchant risk. Through its interventions, the NY Green Bank aims to (i) improve liquidity in the secondary market; and (ii) spur large-scale deployment of renewables by signalling to project developers and financiers that there is enough capital available for new projects to be refinanced and/or acquired.

Source: https://www.cefc.com.au/case-studies/nab-low-carbon-shared-portfolio-opens-up-investment-opportunities/ ;
https://www.iag.com.au/sites/default/files/Documents/Climate%20action/IAG_Climate_Action_Plan_October_2018_1.pdf;
https://www.climatebonds.net/files/files/2018-06%20AU%20NAB%20Trust%20Services%20Limited.pdf;
https://news.nab.com.au/more-investment-in-renewable-energy-projects/;https://greenbank.ny.gov/Investments/Portfolio;
https://greenbanknetwork.org/ny-green-bank/

86 |

Box 3.2. Tools and techniques to mobilise private capital for green infrastructure

The following tables present a typology of risk mitigants and transaction enablers deployed by public actors in G20 countries to catalyse institutional investment in green infrastructure.

Table 3.2. Risk Mitigants

Risk Mitigants	Risk mitigants are defined as either a direct use of public finance or backing a project with public funds which puts public funds at risk. In short, the public actor has a contingent liability.				
		Example			
Name	**Description**	**Project**	**Country**	**Public actor(s) involved**	**Institutional investor**
Co-investment	Public actor(s) invest alongside private investor(s) with either debt or equity with an equal or lower stake than a private investor (any larger investment would be classified as cornerstone stake).	Kathu Concentrated Solar Power Project	South Africa	Development Bank of Southern Africa (DBSA)	Government Employees Pension Fund (GPIC)
Cornerstone stake	Investment by a public actor in a fund, issue or project amounting to a majority equity stake so as to achieve a demonstration effect to attract other investors.	NAB Low Carbon Shared Portfolio Project 1	Australia	Clean Energy Finance Corporation (CEFC) Australia	Insurance Australia Group Ltd., undisclosed institutional investors
Loan	Debt issuance by a public actor	Veja Matte Offshore Wind Farm	Germany	KfW, Bayerische Landesbank, Landesbank Hessen-Thueringen Girozentrale	PensionDanmark A/S and other undisclosed institutional investors through Copenhagen Infrastructure II
Loan guarantee	Guarantee by a public actor to pay any amount (either in full or part) due on a loan in the event of non-payment by the borrower	Walney Island Offshore Wind Farm Extension Phase II	United Kingdom	EKF	PensionDanmark A/S, Pensionskassernes Administration A/S, Legal & General Group PLC Pension Insurance Corp, undisclosed institutional investors through asset management companies
Public seed capital or grants	Concessional fund allocation using public money	SolarReserve Crescent Dunes CSP Plant	United States	United States Department of Energy	Canada's Public Sector Pension Investment Board, Ontario Teachers' Pension Plan
Revenue guarantee	Guarantee by a public actor to pay for the core product to ensure revenue cash flow for a project.	Seine Rive Gauche	France	French Treasury	KGAL Investment Management
Back-stop guarantee	Guarantee by a public actor to purchase any unsubscribed portion of an issue (debt or equity)	Hindustan Solar	India	Asian Development Bank (ADB)	Undisclosed

GREEN INFRASTRUCTURE IN THE DECADE FOR DELIVERY: ASSESSING INSTITUTIONAL INVESTMENT © OECD 2020

| Liquidity facility | A facility by a public actor allowing the borrower to draw thereupon in case of a cash flow shortfall | Thames Tideway Tunnel *(a waste treatment project)* | United Kingdom | Government of United Kingdom | Allianz, Swiss Life Asset Managers, Undisclosed institutional investors through Amber Infrastructure Group, Dalmore Capital Limited |
| Political risk insurance | Guarantee by a public actor to indemnify in case of political risks like currency inconvertibility, expropriation etc. | Elzaig Hospital Campus Project | Turkey | Multilateral Investment Guarantee Agency (MIGA) | Undisclosed |

Table 3.3. Transaction Enablers

Transaction Enablers	*Transaction enablers are defined as interventions by a public entity that do not finance a project directly or put public funds at risk, but facilitate investment from other actors, private or public. Transaction enablers are purely catalytic and no contingent liability is assumed by public funds.*				
		Example			
Name	**Description**	**Project**	**Country**	**Public actor(s) involved**	**Institutional investor**
Warehousing and pooling	Bundling together smaller projects or demand to achieve commercial scale that is attractive and viable for investors.	Tappaghan Mountain Wind Farm	United Kingdom	UK Green Investment Bank	Undisclosed institutional investors through the Greencoat UK Wind PLC
Offtake agreements	Agreements/arrangements with a public actor that has the effect of mitigating project off-take risk (not necessarily for taking off the core product; could also be a renewables quote/certificate).	Kiata Wind Farm	Australia	Government of Victoria	Undisclosed institutional investors through asset management company
Blending	The strategic use of development finance for the mobilisation of additional finance towards sustainable development in developing countries. Note that blending can happen without public funds as well.	PT Royal lestari Utama *(a biodiversity conservation project)*	Indonesia	UN Environment	Undisclosed investors through ADM Capital
Syndication platform	Any mechanism put in place by a public actor to syndicate investments by investors.	SolarVision Celina PV Plant	United Sates	Government of the United States	Undisclosed institutional investors through New energy Capital, Clean Tech Infrastructure Fund

Source: *Adapted from Röttgers, D., A. Tandon and C. Kaminker (2018), "OECD Progress Update on Approaches to Mobilising Institutional Investment for Sustainable Infrastructure", OECD Environment Working Papers, No. 138, OECD Publishing, Paris,* https://doi.org/10.1787/45426991-en

Key takeaways

Based on empirical insights from Chapter 2, this chapter proposes three independent but interlinked pathways for scaling up institutional investment in green infrastructure, in addition to overall climate policy and climate investment incentives: **Green pipelines**, **Mandates** and **Securitised products**.

The **Green pipelines** pathway aims to address the limitation of sufficient investment grade projects. Without a robust pipeline of available infrastructure projects, costs of capacity and skill development are difficult to justify based on one-off investments. Aside from certainty on overall climate policies such as carbon pricing, higher certainty of follow-on projects would allow investors to take calculated risks on investments in these factors. Additionally, a robust pipeline of investment grade projects could help address currently high valuations of projects and therefore allow higher returns, making infrastructure attractive over other investments. It would also allow partnerships of investors to form, which can be effective ways to share risks or otherwise share costs of infrastructure development.

The role of policymakers in building robust pipelines is to provide or support *leadership*, *transparency*, *eligibility criteria*, *project support*, *prioritisation*, and *dynamic adaptability*. Providing risk-mitigation could be particularly useful interventions by public investors. Depending on the state of PFIs in a given jurisdiction, this may require institutional innovation, e.g. adjusting mandates of public financial institutions or forming a new institution like a green investment bank.

The **Mandates** pathway also aims at leveraging the role of asset owners as principals in their relationship with asset managers and investment consultants. Asset owners' mandates form the basis for capital allocation decisions of asset managers and investment consultants. Critical to integrating climate and development objectives in investment decisions is the selection of asset managers and investment consultants. Clarification on the relationship between fiduciary duty, duty of care and consideration of climate-related risks could help greening mandates if permissible from a regulatory point of view.

The **Securitised products** pathway aims at tapping investors with a preference for liquid investment products. Aside from general preferences that asset managers show for liquid investments, securitisation could in particular capitalise on trends towards defined contribution pension plans and passive investment. Securitisation would allow not only to finance infrastructure through liquid products, but also facilitate adjusting to the small scale necessary for these types of investments, in particular to the scale of DC pension plans. YieldCos, and other distribution-based vehicles like infrastructure REITs and INVITs, could be useful instruments in this regard.

To avoid market fragmentation, for securitised products and otherwise, more precise and consistent definitions of which investments are "green" could facilitate investment by giving confidence and assurance to investors. A common understanding, developed in collaboration with industry stakeholders, enables straightforward communication and decision-making regarding investments, accelerating investment flows. The EU Sustainable Finance Taxonomy is the latest example of a policy with this aim.

References

(n.a.) (n.d.), *India Announces a "Green Window" to Catalyze Climate Finance | NRDC*, https://www.nrdc.org/experts/sameer-kwatra/india-announces-green-window-catalyze-climate-finance (accessed on 22 June 2020). [36]

(n.a.) (n.d.), *ROADMAP TO INFRASTRUCTURE AS AN ASSET CLASS Infrastructure for Growth and Development*. [41]

Ang, G., D. Röttgers and P. Burli (2017), "The empirics of enabling investment and innovation in renewable energy", *OECD Environment Working Papers*, No. 123, OECD Publishing, Paris, https://dx.doi.org/10.1787/67d221b8-en. [6]

Bachher, Jagdeep Singh, Adam Dixon, A. (2016), *The New Frontier Investors: How Pension Funds, Sovereign Funds, and Endowments are Changing the Business of Investment Management and Long-Term Investing*. [13]

Blended Finance Taskforce (2018), *Who is the Private Sector? Key Considerations for Mobilising Institutional Capital Through Blended Finance*, https://janike-reichmann-zt7e.squarespace.com/working-papers-1/2018/4/12/who-is-the-private-sector-key-considerations-for-mobilising-institutional-capital-through-blended-finance (accessed on 30 June 2020). [5]

Bloomberg (2019), *How The Asset Management Industry Is Changing*, https://www.bloomberg.com/graphics/2019-asset-management-in-decline/ (accessed on 17 June 2020). [24]

Broadbent, J. and M. Palumbo (2006), *The Shift from Defined Benefit to Defined Contribution Pension Plans-Implications for Asset Allocation and Risk Management*. [21]

Clean Energy Pipeline (2014), *The European Renewable Energy Investor Landscape*, https://www.yumpu.com/en/document/view/47848751/the-european-renewable-energy-investor-landscape (accessed on 16 July 2020). [14]

Climate-Related Market Risk Subcommittee (2020), *Managing Climate Risk in the U.S. Financial System*. [16]

G20/OECD (2013), *High-level principles of long-term investment financing by institutional investors*, http://www.oecd.org (accessed on 18 June 2020). [9]

Halland, H. et al. (2016), *Strategic Investment Funds Opportunities and Challenges*, http://econ.worldbank.org. (accessed on 22 June 2020). [34]

IMF (2018), "Assessing Fiscal Space: An Update and Stocktaking", *IMF Poliy Papers*. [38]

International Monetary Fund (2018), "Assessing Fiscal Space: An Update and Stocktaking", *IMF Policy Papers*. [30]

Kaminker, C. et al. (2013), "Institutional Investors and Green Infrastructure Investments: Selected Case Studies", *OECD Working Papers on Finance, Insurance and Private Pensions*, No. 35, OECD Publishing, Paris, https://dx.doi.org/10.1787/5k3xr8k6jb0n-en. [2]

Kaminker, C., F. Stewart and S. Upton (2012), *The role of institutional investors in financing clean energy*, http://www.oecd.org/sd-roundtable (accessed on 30 June 2020). [4]

KPMG, AIMA, C. (2020), *Sustai nabl e i nvesti ng: fast-forwarding its evolution*, https://assets.kpmg/content/dam/kpmg/xx/pdf/2020/02/sustainable-investing.pdf (accessed on 30 April 2020). [19]

Martini, M. and R. Youngman (2020), "Stocktake of efforts to develop sustainable finance definitions and taxonomies". [25]

Ministry of New and Renewable Energy, Government of India (2019), *IREDA to Create a Green Window for Green Energy Finance:Shri Anand Kumar*, https://pib.gov.in/newsite/PrintRelease.aspx?relid=195728 (accessed on 22 June 2020). [33]

Morningstar (2020), *Surge in Funds Rebranding as Sustainable | Morningstar*, https://www.morningstar.co.uk/uk/news/201590/surge-in-funds-rebranding-as-sustainable.aspx (accessed on 17 June 2020). [18]

NAPA (2019), *Retirement Assets Top $29 Trillion, While Plan Fees Continue Downward Trend | National Association of Plan Advisors*, https://www.napa-net.org/news-info/daily-news/retirement-assets-top-29-trillion-while-plan-fees-continue-downward-trend (accessed on 23 June 2020). [22]

Nelson, D. and B. Pierpont (2013), *The Challenge of Institutional Investment in Renewable Energy CPI Report Climate Policy Initiative*, http://www.climatepolicyinitiative.org (accessed on 24 June 2020). [37]

Nelson, D. and B. Pierpont (2013), "The Challenge of Institutional Investment in Renewable Energy CPI Report Climate Policy Initiative". [3]

OECD (2020), *The Role of Sovereign and Strategic Investment Funds in the Low-carbon Transition*, OECD Development Policy Tools, OECD Publishing, Paris, https://dx.doi.org/10.1787/ddfd6a9f-en. [35]

OECD (2018), *Developing Robust Project Pipelines for Low-Carbon Infrastructure*, Green Finance and Investment, OECD Publishing, Paris, https://dx.doi.org/10.1787/9789264307827-en. [8]

OECD (2017), *Green Investment Banks Innovative Public Financial Institutions Scaling up Private, Low-carbon Investment*, https://doi.org/10.1787/9789264245129-en (accessed on 22 June 2020). [31]

OECD (2017), "Green Investment Banks: Innovative Public Financial Institutions Scaling up Private, Low-carbon Investment", *OECD Environment Policy Papers*, No. 6, OECD Publishing, Paris, https://dx.doi.org/10.1787/e3c2526c-en. [40]

OECD (2017), *Investing in Climate, Investing in Growth*, OECD Publishing, Paris, https://dx.doi.org/10.1787/9789264273528-en. [7]

OECD (2016), *Green Investment Banks: Scaling Up Private Investment in Low-carbon, Climate-resilient Infrastructure*, OECD Publishing, Paris, http://dx.doi.org/10.1787/9789264245129-en (accessed on 24 September 2018). [10]

OECD (2016), *Green Investment Banks: Scaling up Private Investment in Low-carbon, Climate-resilient Infrastructure*, Green Finance and Investment, OECD Publishing, Paris, https://dx.doi.org/10.1787/9789264245129-en. [32]

OECD (2015), *Mapping Channels to Mobilise Institutional Investment in Sustainable Energy*, Green Finance and Investment, OECD Publishing, Paris, https://dx.doi.org/10.1787/9789264224582-en. [1]

OECD (2015), *Policy Guidance for Investment in Clean Energy Infrastructure: Expanding Access to Clean Energy for Green Growth and Development*, OECD Publishing, Paris, https://dx.doi.org/10.1787/9789264212664-en. [39]

Prequin (2020), *Preqin Quarterly Update: Infrastructure, Q1 2020*, https://www.preqin.com/insights/research/quarterly-updates/preqin-quarterly-update-infrastructure-q1-202 (accessed on 17 June 2020). [12]

PRI (2018), *An investor initiative in partnership with UNEP Finance Initiative and UN Global Compact PRINCIPLES FOR RESPONSIBLE INVESTMENT Annual Report 2018*. [17]

PRI (2017), *An investor initiative in partnership with UNEP Finance Initiative and UN Global Compact INVESTMENT CONSULTANT SERVICES REVIEW WORKING TOWARDS A SUSTAINABLE FINANCIAL SYSTEM*, http://www.unpri.org/sfs (accessed on 19 June 2020). [20]

Röttgers, D., A. Tandon and C. Kaminker (2018), "OECD Progress Update on Approaches to Mobilising Institutional Investment for Sustainable Infrastructure", *OECD Environment Working Papers*, No. 138, OECD Publishing, Paris, https://dx.doi.org/10.1787/45426991-en. [27]

Roy, R., A. Heuty and E. Letouzé (2007), *FISCAL SPACE FOR WHAT? ANALYTICAL ISSUES FROM A HUMAN DEVELOPMENT PERSPECTIVE 1*, https://books.google.fr/books?hl=fr&lr=&id=KXoYmQqGtPMC&oi=fnd&pg=PA31&dq=Fiscal+space+for+what%3F+Analytical+issues+from+a+human+development+perspective.&ots=Q7W27q5h3O&sig=cfiipxgIQFWMo1bFBucaEGWlrA8 (accessed on 30 June 2020). [29]

Task Force on Climate-related Financial Disclosure (2017), *Recommendations of the Task Force on Climate-related Financial Disclosures i Letter from Michael R. Bloomberg*. [26]

UBS (2019), *Top infrastructure trends for 2020 | UBS Global topics*, https://www.ubs.com/global/en/asset-management/insights/asset-class-research/real-assets/2019/top-infrastructure-trends-for-2020.html (accessed on 17 June 2020). [11]

UNEP FI, PRI (2019), *FIDUCIARY DUTY IN THE 21ST CENTURY*, https://www.unepfi.org/wordpress/wp-content/uploads/2019/10/Fiduciary-duty-21st-century-final-report.pdf (accessed on 25 June 2020). [15]

Wai, H., J. Cheng and I. Pitterle (2018), *Towards a more comprehensive assessment of fiscal space*, https://www.un.org/development/ (accessed on 30 June 2020). [28]

Wilshire Funds Management (2016), *INCOME-ORIENTED RETIREMENT PORTFOLIOS: CHALLENGES AND SOLUTIONS*, https://www.ebri.org/pdf/ (accessed on 25 June 2020). [23]

Notes

[1] Analysis in this report should not be misconstrued as investment advice.

[2] Unless stated otherwise, the term YieldCo in this report refers generally to the legal structure that enables securitising illiquid physical assets, and not to any particular vehicle or strategy in existence in the market either presently or at any time in the past.

[3] A private placement is a direct sale of securities to an investor, as opposed to a sale at public markets.

[4] Across all infrastructure strategies, i.e. core (very low risk portfolio), core plus (low to moderate risk), value-add (moderate to high risk), and opportunistic (very high risk); authors' calculations based on Preqin (2020).

[5] Authors' calculations based on Preqin (2020).

[6] OECD publications on policy frameworks to enable investment includes but is not limited to OECD (2015[39]), Ang, Röttgers and Burli (2017[6]), OECD (2018[8]), OECD (2016[10]). Initiatives aimed at addressing the challenge include the Climate Investment Platform (https://www.climateinvestmentplatform.com/).

[7] Examples of such initiatives include Blended Finance Taskforce, Climate Investment Platform, Closing the Investment Gap, and FAST-Infra (formerly VERT-Infra; see also below).

[8] Excluding collective defined contribution plans

[9] Investment decisions are delegated to a trustee in the case of *collective* defined contribution plans.

[10] Distribution-based vehicles generally distribute most or all of the operational cash-flow to shareholders.

[11] https://www.climatefinancelab.org/about/how-it-works/

[12] https://www.scalingsolar.org/news/

[13] https://www.weforum.org/agenda/2020/09/how-to-drive-investment-into-sustainable-infrastructure/

www.ingramcontent.com/pod-product-compliance
Lightning Source LLC
Chambersburg PA
CBHW082108210326
41599CB00033B/6636